Exploring Careers in Music

2nd Edition

MENC: The National Association for Music Education

MENC: The National Association for Music Education is grateful to all of the organizations and individuals who assisted in compiling this book.

Special thanks to Irma Collins, Michael George, Marvelene Moore, David Peters, Richard Sang, Schott Shuler, and Wendy Sims.

Compiled by
Kate Bohonos and Evonne Tvardek

This book is a revised and expanded version of
Exploring Careers in Music, First Edition, published jointly by MENC and the American Music Conference (AMC) in 1990.

Contents

Introduction

If you are considering a career in music, you've opened the right book. *Exploring Careers in Music,* 2nd edition, is full of helpful information about a multitude of music careers. You will find insightful job descriptions and valuable advice written by successful professionals in the fields of music education, performance, music business, music communications, the recording industry, music technology, and even music and health care!

At one time, these professionals found themselves in a position similar to the one you are in today. First, they had to decide whether music was to be their life's work or a favorite pastime and possible secondary source of income. Once it was established that they wanted to enter the field of music, these enterprising individuals had to choose a specific career path and then work diligently in order to reach their goals. The experience of the contributors will help you make sound choices regarding your future.

While a music profession requires extreme dedication and self-discipline, a career in music can be very satisfying. As you work in the field, you will likely find yourself working with others who share your passion for music, which will foster artistic growth in all involved. And whether you work as a teacher, a performer, or any other music professional, you can be assured that you will have a direct impact on society and culture. You may help preserve the rich heritage of music, and you may make history by taking part in exciting musical innovations. Whichever music career you choose, you will probably one day serve as an inspiration to a budding young musician. The possibilities are endless.

It is recommended that you familiarize yourself with all of the job descriptions included in this book. A career that you have not yet considered may be your dream job! After you have chosen a career area on which to focus, get in touch with professionals in the field. They will be able to tell you about tricks of the trade and the best places to study. Also talk to your music teacher, college music educator, or career counselor, and contact the appropriate associations listed at the end of this book for further information. Look for internships through school or professional organizations, or on your own. Do everything you can to explore the career that you are considering so that you can make an informed decision.

Remember that you need not pursue a career in music in order to stay involved in music. Likewise, a career in a nonperformance sector of music does not dictate that you will no longer be able to perform. From freelancing as an artist who performs for weddings and special occasions to participating in a community ensemble, you will always be able to find opportunities for performance.

Enjoy your exploration of career options. Use the information in the pages that follow as a starting point. While it is virtually impossible to include each and every music-related job (many people invent their own positions!), this book is an ideal resource with which to begin.

Music
Education

Music education begins at birth and continues throughout life. That which individuals learn in the classroom becomes a prime influence on the musical vitality of communities and the nation. Music educators instill and foster musical understanding and skill in students both young and old. The profession of music education is a challenging one, but one that offers a large measure of personal stimulation and gratification.

Music educators must be accomplished musicians and have a well-developed philosophy of music and education. They should demonstrate a familiarity with educational thought and be able to apply a broad knowledge of musical repertoire to the learning problems of music students. They must be flexible and open to innovation and expanding concepts.

A degree in music education is necessary for all music teachers. Undergraduate music education degrees are offered in many forms, including Bachelor of Arts, Bachelor of Science, and Bachelor of Music. According to the National Association of Schools of Music, the differences between various types of degrees lie in the percentage of music and nonmusic courses in a given program.

The term "music education" covers a spectrum of specializations, many of which will be explored in the following chapter.

School Music Educator

Early Childhood Music Educator

Prekindergarten music education can involve children from birth to five years of age. The most common age-group served by early childhood music teachers is three- to five-year-olds; however, music classes attended by infants and toddlers together with a parent are becoming increasingly popular. Most prekindergarten music teaching takes place in preschools and day care centers, and is often conducted by the teaching staff rather than by a music specialist. This is changing slowly, however, with some centers hiring full-time music teachers and a greater number hiring freelance music teachers who travel from one school to another to work with the children several times a week, perhaps also serving as consultants to the school staff and parents. Public schools are beginning to offer preschool classes for four-year-olds, often as part of early-intervention programs for children from disadvantaged backgrounds, with developmental delays, or with other special needs. In these programs, music is often included in the curriculum and is taught by a music specialist.

Recent publicity about the importance of music in early childhood has also resulted in the rapid expansion of private music classes for young children. Some music teachers develop their own programs, while some work with private music studios or university music schools.

Music programs for prekindergarten should not be conducted in the same way that elementary school music programs are—they must be specially designed to meet the developmental needs of younger children. Appropriate programs are play-based, rather than performance-based, and include singing, moving, listening, playing instruments, creating, and responding. The goal is for the young child to develop a positive attitude toward music, while at the same time acquiring knowledge and skills that serve as a foundation upon which future music learning will be built.

Elementary Music Educator
Teaching music in elementary schools presents a challenging and rewarding opportunity either in a full- or part-time position. Most school districts and many states have adopted specific music standards for their students and teachers to meet, and many have developed standards for assessing student performance. These standards are often the basis of a general music course in which teachers give students a broad background in musical literacy in preparation for later instruction in the performing arts. Commonly, the elementary curriculum tends to be eclectic and frequently includes approaches developed by educators such as Zoltán Kodály, Carl Orff, Emile Jaques-Dalcroze, Edwin Gordon, and Shinichi Suzuki, as well as the teaching of comprehensive musicianship. Often, the curriculum centers on a basal music series.

In many communities, there is an elementary general music teacher in each school who is responsible for music instruction and activities; in other communities, one teacher may visit several schools. In some systems, children may come to a music room, while in others the general music teacher goes to individual classrooms. The general music teacher is often responsible for leading choral groups in addition to teaching general music.

Instrumental teachers are responsible for recruiting students into their program, providing instruction to beginners on various instruments, conducting ensembles, and promoting and developing instrumental programs. Sometimes, they also teach general music classes. An instrumental teacher may teach in one school or divide his or her time between two or more schools.

In some elementary schools, class piano is offered. Sometimes the teacher is a piano specialist, but this responsibility is often handled by a general music teacher or instrumental instructor.

All of these positions may be itinerant in nature, with teachers visiting more than one school each week, and all require the ability to communicate effectively and persuasively with different administrators and numerous classroom teachers.

In some school systems, elementary music is taught by the classroom teacher under the guidance of a music specialist. In this case, the specialist plans and guides music learning experiences and assists the classroom teacher. This may include demonstration lessons and regularly scheduled teaching in the classroom.

In other systems, the specialist serves as a resource person, locating music materials and coordinating music activities that are integrated with school programs and academic areas. When teachers assume the role of specialist or coordinator, they also need administrative skills, since they are part of the administrative staff. Especially important is the ability to work with people.

Junior or Senior High Music Educator

In many smaller school systems, the music teacher has a joint junior/senior high or elementary/junior high appointment, which may include a combination of vocal and instrumental music instruction. Larger systems usually have both a vocal and an instrumental teacher for each school.

The vocal music teacher is normally responsible for the general music class in addition to the school choir and vocal ensembles. The general music class provides opportunities for students to create, understand, and respond to music, and does not stress performance. It often includes opportunities for students to sing and perform on instruments, however. Teachers must be prepared to instruct students in the tradition of Western classical music as well as multicultural, jazz, rock, folk, and popular contemporary music.

In some cases, where the school population is too small to support a teacher in both vocal and instrumental music, or where it may be so large that it requires three or four teachers, assignments may overlap. An instrumentalist might teach general music or chorus; a vocalist with an instrumental proficiency might teach a single family of instruments. In systems with declining enrollment, a music teacher may be called on to teach other subjects as well. In large senior high schools with several music staff members, there is usually a band director, an orchestra director, and a choral director. Sometimes, instrumental teachers in the same school district, who specialize in certain families of instruments (strings, woodwinds, brass, or percussion), divide teaching responsibilities among themselves so that each can concentrate teaching efforts on his or her area of specialization.

Senior high school music electives may include music theory, music appreciation, music history and literature, general music, music in combination with other arts (for example, a related arts course), composition, voice classes, and small ensembles. Some schools offer guitar classes and have specialized performance groups such as steel band ensembles and mariachi bands. Staff members are assigned to these courses according to their training and experience.

The vocal specialist in junior and senior high schools should have voice training and choral conducting experience. The ability to play piano is required when an accompanist is not available for rehearsals or when coaching voice. Many high schools have a mixed choir, separate boys' and girls' choirs, a show choir, a jazz choir, a gospel choir, or any combination of these, all of which may come under the direction of the choral music teacher.

Because instrumental music is an elective subject in most schools, instrumental teachers must be able to recruit and instruct beginning talent. In many situations, the instrumental teacher must be equipped to teach wind, string, and percussion instruments, although some school systems may have specialists in these areas. Many schools offer both orchestra and band programs, and it is necessary for instrumental teachers to be able to instruct and conduct such ensembles. Instrumental instructors also should be prepared to teach jazz programs, which have become more and more a part of the regular curriculum. The ability to arrange music for particular ensembles is also a valuable skill.

Skills and Preparation
In the United States, there is no central agency for licensing teachers. Each state sets its own requirements and issues necessary licenses to teach within its borders. However, states generally agree on qualifications and there is a great deal of reciprocity. To be certain,

teachers should go to the appropriate state department of education for information about licensing or certification requirements. The music education department at any college or university also may help in determining certification requirements for a specific state.

Prekindergarten music educators above all should love and respect young children. They should possess a high level of musicianship and be able to improvise both musically and instructionally. Although they must be able to plan, model, and guide appropriate musical experiences, they should be flexible and able to adapt to children's needs.

The preparation of prekindergarten music educators should include training in child development and developmentally appropriate music teaching practice. Courses and workshops in music for early childhood are becoming more readily available in community colleges, four-year colleges, and universities.

Any elementary music teacher should be able to play and improvise on the piano or the guitar. He or she should have a trained ear that will perceive pitch and interval variances so students can develop a degree of pitch discernment as well as find their singing voices. Furthermore, a teacher needs to develop a singing voice that will be an example for the children to emulate. Even more essential is a clear understanding of children's vocal and pitch development and of good literature.

Secondary school teachers have to be able to identify with the adolescent learner, who is undergoing physical and psychological changes. Changing voices must be taken into consideration when choosing vocal repertoire. Also, music teachers must realize the importance of their role in secondary students' lives. Music can help students nearing adulthood to develop close ties with the community.

Prospective teachers have the responsibility to expand their experiences and their knowledge beyond the discipline chosen for their career. Music education students must grow intellectually through the study of liberal arts and sciences that constitute our broad cultural heritage. Through these experiences, they develop resources, understandings, and personal skills from which to draw for future growth. The diversity of such experiences allows the student to struggle with new models for thinking—in both traditional and developing disciplines. Furthermore, it can foster the development of intelligent decisions regarding the role of music in our society and in making judgments about the quality of musical literature and performance. Therefore, intellectually, the prospective music teacher should do the following:

- expand personal curiosity for learning itself and not be confined to a specific discipline
- develop a personal philosophy of music education
- discover new intellectual resources that challenge traditional viewpoints
- apply the skills of critical thinking to daily problem solving
- investigate the use and value of music in various societies
- develop an understanding of the related arts and various theories of aesthetic meaning
- seek to understand and respect diversity in individuals and ideas

Most music students enter college with a considerable background in music performance. The college program expands those experiences by providing formal course work for the acquisition of musical knowledge and the development of personal skills as the student makes a mature commitment to the profession. Through the process of becoming familiar with their own musical performance, creativity, and understanding, prospective music teachers must learn to see how all musical experiences combine to prepare them for teaching.

The applied lessons, classes, and performing ensembles provide model settings through which music education students gain understanding of performance problems, active listening, musical analysis, rehearsal design, conducting, and class planning. Through these daily contacts, ideas and techniques for teaching music are perceived and reinforced. From a musical growth perspective, the prospective music teacher should do the following while studying music education:

- demonstrate skill in listening, analyzing, notating, arranging, composing, improvising, performing, rehearsing, and evaluating
- understand the broad relationships among musical styles, musical forms, historical periods, and composers
- investigate the artistic and sociopolitical influences found in the music that is studied
- apply qualitative criteria in making judgments about the music selected for study and performance

- develop analytical procedures based on an aural perception of music that go beyond sets of rules and non-sound-oriented techniques
- utilize technology to practice and develop ear training, sight singing, and other skills that translate notation into music in an accurate and artistic fashion
- integrate the understandings gained from his or her training (including music history, theory, performance, and creative activities) into the providing of musical experiences for all music classes (including solo, chamber, and large-ensemble performance classes) and into determining performance practice
- develop creative skills for use in performance
- develop sight-reading skills in order to have the ability to learn new music quickly, accompany others, and transpose music at sight
- demonstrate knowledge of instrumental or vocal pedagogy and performance practice by modeling on piano, fretted classroom instruments, secondary instruments, and with voice
- detect errors in performance and demonstrate the correct response

Most young music students require the expertise and assistance of a well-prepared music teacher if they are to understand and demonstrate personal mastery of the subject. Some students may learn regardless of the quality of the guidance; most, however, benefit from systematic and insightful leadership. Formal courses in education and special methods courses in music education must assist the teacher candidate in developing the myriad skills and knowledge that can help students learn music. Formal course work must be matched with opportunities for practical application of theories and good principles of instruction. The process of learning how to teach should place the prospective teacher in a variety of teaching and learning settings throughout the teacher certification program. From a pedagogical perspective, there are many things a prospective music teacher should do while studying music education:

- demonstrate understanding of the theories of sensation, attention, perception, growth and development, motivation, and other aspects of human behavior
- apply knowledge regarding the cognitive, affective, and psychomotor domains of learning to instruction planning
- seek answers to instructional problems from appropriate research

- explore the use of personal, intellectual, musical, and instructional resources in peer and small-group instruction and in on-site classroom and rehearsal observations
- become knowledgeable about the National Standards for Music Education and state standards and about how to develop a standards-based music curriculum (MENC: The National Association for Music Education has published materials to assist teachers with planning and implementing music curricula)
- perceive and evaluate evidence of unique learning styles and varied stages and levels of learning as they are observed in field experience
- develop the capacity to make intelligent decisions for sequencing instruction
- demonstrate a practical understanding of a variety of teaching techniques and methodologies
- develop an understanding of the effective evaluation of learning and teaching
- demonstrate effective skills in written, spoken, and musical communication
- develop an understanding of the philosophical viewpoints regarding the discipline of music education
- employ educational technology in a manner that enhances the effectiveness of learning for individual students

Getting a Job

The more specific the field of music in which one wishes to teach, the more flexible one must be with respect to *where* one is willing to teach. If a teacher wants to conduct choirs exclusively, he or she should keep in mind there are few such assignments. Most vocal teachers work in related fields such as general music, voice classes, theory, or even other subject areas in addition to directing choirs. Instrumental assignments in senior high schools often involve a combination of theory, music appreciation, and other subjects as well.

The nature of the job market will also affect employment prospects, as it varies considerably from state to state and even within states. Any capable teacher who is willing to work in a geographic area that has a shortage of teachers (such as inner cities or rural communities) will most likely find a job.

When seeking employment in areas where there are special considerations or problems, one must not only be knowledgeable about his or her subject but also be able to cope with unusual situations. An educator in such situations should have some background in sociology and psychology. It is especially desirable to do student teaching where similar conditions prevail.

To get a job in a particular part of the country, one should apply through school district personnel offices in surrounding communities as well as in the specific location in which one wishes to teach. Nearly all universities have placement bureaus, and while these agencies are effective, one should not rely on them entirely. Other resources include one's college's music education faculty, state music associations, and MENC.

It is important to remember that the perfect job does not exist. When applying for a position, a music educator should be prepared to assume obligations that may not always be at the top of his or her priorities.

There are some key things to keep in mind when preparing for an interview. Most interviewers are interested in how their applicant thinks and his or her musical abilities. When interviewing or being considered as a candidate for a music teaching job, in addition to the appropriate documentation (such as a bachelor's or master's degree, state teacher certification, letters of recommendation, and college academic records), one should expect to demonstrate a number of skills or activities.

Usually the focus of the interview or audition is based on the job being filled. For example, for an elementary school job, one might be asked to play a simple song accompaniment on piano or guitar. Applying for a senior high school orchestra position may require that the applicant perform on his or her major instrument or conduct an ensemble. It is not out of line to ask beforehand about the nature of the interview and the audition if one is required. Interviews not only help the employer learn more about the applicant, but also help the applicant learn about the position.

According to *Music Teacher Education: Partnership and Process,* a report from the MENC Teacher Education Task Force (published in

1987 by MENC) and other sources, the music educator may be evaluated on the following skills and activities:

Instructional Skills
- teach a lesson that illustrates knowledge of lesson planning
- conduct a rehearsal that demonstrates good rehearsal technique and preparation
- teach or conduct a lesson that demonstrates effective classroom management
- teach or conduct a lesson that illustrates knowledge of a variety of learning needs
- teach or conduct a lesson that demonstrates vocal projection, appropriate grammar, self-confidence, and general deportment
- teach or conduct a lesson that demonstrates the ability to motivate students toward musical learning and appreciation
- pass a state or national teacher-competency exam if required by the employing agency

Musical Skills
- perform a composition to demonstrate musical sensitivity
- perform in a secondary medium (piano, guitar, voice, classroom or other secondary instrument) in a teaching context of the position being sought
- teach or conduct a lesson that demonstrates knowledge of music history, music theory, music composition, and creativity
- teach or conduct a lesson that demonstrates how musical listening affects musical learning
- teach or conduct a lesson that illustrates the ability to hear musical performance problems and prescribe solutions
- pass a state or national subject-matter competency exam if required by the employing agency

Personal Abilities
- demonstrate the degree to which professional goals have been determined
- demonstrate the nature of commitment to teaching music
- show an understanding of the development of personal relationships with students, colleagues, administrators, parents, and community members
- demonstrate the development of a philosophy of music education

The career of a music educator is constantly challenging, but consistently rewarding as well. Teaching music is a wonderful way to make a living.

Compiled by MENC: The National Association for Music Education with the assistance of the National Association of Schools of Music.

College/University Professor

A college music faculty member must have excellent performance, communication, and organizational skills. All faculty are required to demonstrate advanced musical skills in a variety of settings, to write for publication in refereed journals, and to participate in many committee activities requiring verbal and written communication skills.

The faculty member whose primary appointment is in applied music must give regular recitals, write for publication in a relevant music journal, and actively participate in student recruitment. If the appointment includes ensemble work, there is usually a required minimum of two concerts a year. College music teaching is intensely demanding, yet it is very satisfying as a professional career.

Skills and Preparation

Teaching at the college level requires basic competencies beyond undergraduate preparation—in most cases, beyond completion of a master's degree, approaching the completion of a doctorate. If candidates have developed performance skills along with an international reputation, an appointment as an artist faculty member is possible without a doctorate.

College teaching appointments vary according to the size of the department, school, or college of music. Music education professors may teach any aspect of a music education undergraduate curriculum and some graduate classes. Student teacher and intern observation is usually a part of the faculty load.

Compiled with the assistance of The College Music Society.

Music Supervisor

In large communities, the supervision of classroom instruction is often a responsibility of music supervisors. These individuals spend much of their time working with teachers, parents, and other administrators. They review teaching techniques, provide in-service training courses for classroom teachers, evaluate instruction, and coordinate large district or city programs.

A music supervisor should enjoy working with both adults and children and have a personality that instills confidence and elicits cooperation from the staff. He or she also should possess a level of musical ability that commands the respect of the community's musicians. With these qualities, a supervisor will enhance the overall position of music in the school system.

Music supervisors can work at the district or state level. The total number of state education departments or agencies that employ a specialist to oversee music education has increased, but the scope of many of these positions has been expanded to include all of the arts rather than focusing solely on music. As a result, there are fewer state supervisors whose background is specifically in music, and an increasing number whose background is in other art forms, particularly the visual arts. The title "state supervisor of music" has in many states been replaced by the title "state music consultant" to reflect a role that has become more supportive than directive, or even "state arts consultant" to reflect a broadened scope.

State music or arts consultants assist state departments of education as they make recommendations to and carry out the policies of state legislatures and state boards of education. State supervisors of music also serve as liaisons between disciplines, helping coordinate music with other subject fields in curricular matters. They take the lead in setting standards for classroom instruction; enforcing, designing, and implementing curricula; and evaluating programs and students. They keep music teachers informed of current developments in music education, are available for consultation, and give advice about expanding music programs and improving instruction.

When selecting state supervisors of music, committees usually seek individuals with years of successful teaching experience in a variety of situations. For positions devoted specifically to music, search committees typically prefer someone with experience teaching at all grade levels and in both vocal and instrumental music; for positions devoted to all of the arts, committees tend to look for someone involved in more than one art form. Many state music or arts consultants have earned doctoral degrees in their field. Because these positions are dependent upon funds allocated by state legislatures, state supervisors do not always receive a salary commensurate with their experience and responsibilities, and the scope of their work often changes.

Skills and Preparation
As in any administrative position, state music supervisors must possess skills in working with people, with a particular emphasis on working collaboratively with other adults; have expertise in curriculum development at the local level; be skilled musicians and teachers; understand trends in their content area(s) and in education; and be capable of inspiring both laypersons and music teachers to understand and embrace the important role of music in education. They should have the breadth to see music as part of the total educational experience, the patience to see projects evolve over long periods of time, and the willingness to share or even forego credit for significant accomplishments so that those accomplishments can be viewed as statewide successes.

Compiled by MENC:The National Association for Music Education.

Independent Teacher

Working in a school setting is not the only option for those interested in teaching music. Another option to consider is teaching privately. Well-qualified, dedicated, independent music teachers are in demand in many geographic areas.

Independent teachers have the satisfaction of sharing their vocal or instrumental music mastery with others while being their own bosses. The schedule is flexible; it can be a full-time career or a part-time means of supplementing income. Independent teachers plan their own schedules so that their work week can be as long or as short as they like. They can work out of their homes or rent a studio in another location, such as a small retail store or a church.

Opportunities for full-time independent teachers vary from place to place. Early childhood is a growing field for independent teachers throughout the United States. In areas of the country with few or no school music programs, there is a strong demand for private lessons. In communities with strong school band, orchestra, and choral programs, the sheer number of students involved often prevents the director from providing sufficient individual attention. Lessons on a one-to-one basis can be a valuable supplement to school programs. Before setting up shop, one should be sure to check out the competition in the area; a specialty may already be taught by several others.

There is greatest demand for piano, organ, and guitar teachers. These are the most popular instruments among America's amateur musicians and are not taught as part of the school music curriculum as often as band and orchestral instruments are. Teenagers and young adults tend to have a particularly strong interest in the guitar, so qualified teachers have little trouble attracting students. Private string teachers are also in demand, particularly in areas near clusters of school string programs.

In the past, parents who wanted to introduce children to music often began with providing piano lessons, because lessons could be started at an earlier age than lessons for most other instruments. Today, the availability of appropriately sized instruments and the Suzuki approach to instruction makes piano, stringed instruments, flute, and other instruments accessible to even very young children.

Recent trends have also shown that many adults are taking lessons with an eye toward developing proficiency on an instrument, possibly one they studied in childhood. This group of students includes some of the most dedicated and interested pupils and now constitutes a large and growing market.

Many music stores have instrumental or vocal instruction programs that employ independent teachers (see "Retailer" on page 58). In some cases, the teachers are salaried employees and also serve on the sales staff or as teaching program coordinators. In other instances, teachers may rent studio space from the store and collect their own fees from the students. Some use in-store space free of charge.

Many independent teachers explore group instructional methods, which are especially applicable to teaching piano, guitar, and stringed instruments. Some teachers find group instruction more challenging and more lucrative than one-on-one teaching. Before entering a group teaching situation, a music teacher should investigate the large number of commercially available lesson programs and curricula and decide whether to use an existing method or create a new one. Group guitar lessons can easily be organized in a private home; all that is needed is a well-lit space, a blackboard, and some folding chairs. Group piano, of course, requires more than one instrument and may limit the choice of lesson space.

Many programs combine the best attributes of both private and group lessons into a curriculum that provides total musicianship, including performance skills, theory, ear training, improvisation, and composition. Also, independent teachers are exploring the incorporation of modern technology—computer-assisted instruction, synthesizers, and electronic keyboards—into their instructional programs.

Skills and Preparation

To succeed as an independent music teacher, one must give attention to musical, educational, and pedagogical development. An independent teacher should get the best training possible and continue to seek out learning opportunities throughout his or her career. An independent teacher should also know the capabilities of his or her instrument or voice and be able to demonstrate them. The more versatile one is, the better the chances of success.

In addition to being a good musician and keeping musically active, an independent teacher must have an aptitude for teaching and be able to do it with enthusiasm. To be a good teacher, he or she must have patience and enjoy the creative process of helping students grow as musicians.

Many colleges offer courses and degrees in pedagogy, which provide a valuable background for independent teachers. It is usually desirable for an independent music teacher to have a degree in music from a college or conservatory, but one who has extensive performing experience may also be qualified to teach.

An ability to accomplish musical objectives quickly and successfully is necessary. Some of the prerequisites of independent teaching include the following:

- knowledge of child (and general human) development, stages of learning, and learning styles
- familiarity with the teaching materials and repertoire available for the level(s) of students to be taught
- a knowledge of music history, stylistic considerations, compositional techniques, and music theory
- ability to communicate in a concise, understandable fashion
- reasonable proficiency in playing many types of music and in sight-reading
- ability to adjust teaching style to the needs of the individual student

In addition to a thorough knowledge of pedagogy and his or her area of specialization, an independent music teacher must be educated in common business practices. Conducting a studio in a professional manner by keeping records for tax purposes and making wise decisions about equipment and materials is part of successful studio teaching. Also, it is necessary to know and understand the laws (tax, zoning, insurance, etc.) that regulate small businesses.

Good teachers always remain students themselves, staying on top of new developments in their field and searching constantly for ways to improve their teaching. Although the profession of independent teaching is flexible and self-regulating in terms of class size, kind of students, type of studio, and size of income, this fact should not in any way detract from the necessity for full- and part-time independent teachers to continue to grow professionally. For support, independent music teachers join professional music organizations to associate with fellow teachers. They attend workshops and clinics and subscribe to professional journals to keep informed about new teaching methods and materials.

Compiled with the assistance of the American String Teachers Association with National School Orchestra Association and the Music Teachers National Association.

Music
Performance

The field of professional music performance is highly competitive. Still, many are drawn to it—some for the rush of adrenaline that is experienced just before a performance, and others for the enjoyment of creating and sharing music with others. Performance opportunities exist for people with talent, regardless of their career choice. Since many ensembles practice in the evenings and on weekends, a music teacher or someone who works at an office job from nine to five can be a member of a professional or community choir, orchestra, band, or jazz ensemble. Composers can write their music whenever they have free time. In the pages that follow, you will find information about careers that can serve as part- or full-time endeavors.

Orchestra Performer

From part-time work with largely volunteer community and youth orchestras to full-time employment with professional ensembles, American orchestras provide a wide range of job opportunities.

Major orchestras offer musicians and principal players full-time employment. Most metropolitan orchestras have seasons of forty or fifty-two weeks, which may include youth concerts, tours, and summer or pops engagements, in addition to the regular concert series.

Orchestras with small budgets generally employ musicians on a weekly basis, a per-service basis, or a combination of both. Organizations in this category differ widely in the numbers and types of concerts they perform. They often perform chamber and ensemble concerts in addition to full-orchestra concerts. As few as ten or as many as one hundred performances a year may be given by the full orchestra.

Some of these orchestras employ a core ensemble or quartet on a full-time basis and augment it with musicians hired on a per-service basis to accommodate the larger symphonic repertoire. Others may retain a full-size orchestra on a limited-season contract and divide personnel for various services. Professional chamber orchestras generally have longer seasons and pay higher salaries than full symphony orchestras.

Most urban and community orchestras with budgets under $250,000 hire musicians on a per-service basis, and annual earnings depend on the number of concerts given. Most musicians in these orchestras hold other full-time jobs or supplement their income with independent teaching. In large metropolitan areas, some manage a good wage by playing with several small community and chamber orchestras. Occasionally these part-time orchestra positions are offered in conjunction with college or school faculty positions. Community orchestras may pay musicians on a per-service basis or may pay only section leaders and concertmasters, with the rest of the musicians being volunteers.

Skills and Preparation

Professional symphony musicians need years of private instrumental study before they begin conservatory-level training. While completion of a degree program is not essential, most orchestra musicians today have conservatory or university training.

It is wise to get as much ensemble experience as possible before entering college. Youth orchestras and summer music camps offer excellent opportunities for that. Apprenticeships with smaller semiprofessional orchestras can also help in expanding orchestral repertoire before auditioning for a professional position.

The Tanglewood Music Center's Summer Fellowship Program in Lenox, Massachusetts, offers young instrumentalists intensive instruction in orchestral and chamber music and an opportunity to work with well-known musicians. All students chosen to participate in the program receive full fellowships covering tuition and room and board.

Interlochen Arts Camp provides training on all orchestral and band instruments for students ages eight through high school during its eight-week summer program. The camp offers many performance opportunities, an extensive study of music literature, and exposure to great artists and other arts areas. Interlochen Arts Academy, a college preparatory high school with a fine arts emphasis, offers training in all forms of music and provides performance opportunities on the Interlochen campus and on tour.

The Aspen Music School offers an opportunity to play with a variety of orchestral ensembles during four-and-a-half-week or nine-week sessions each summer. The Festival Orchestra and the Chamber Symphony consist of professional faculty and students. The Aspen Sinfonia, Concert Orchestra, and the American Academy of

Conducting Orchestra are all formed from the student body. Students may attend classes in music literature and theory and take private instrumental lessons and master classes from noted performers. Instruction in orchestral performance practice is offered for students in all instrument groups. Chamber music courses are also offered. More than 70 percent of Aspen students receive some financial assistance.

Many American universities and conservatories are well known for training orchestral musicians, among them the Eastman School of Music, the Manhattan School of Music, the Conservatory of Music at Oberlin College, The Juilliard School, The Curtis Institute, New England Conservatory, Indiana University, Yale University, the Cleveland Institute, the Shepherd School of Music at Rice University, and the College-Conservatory of Music at the University of Cincinnati. In addition, training is available at orchestras such as the New World Symphony in Miami, Florida, and Young Musicians Foundation Debut Orchestra in Los Angeles, and through extracurricular opportunities at summer music camps provided by a variety of groups.

Compiled with the assistance of the American String Teachers Association with National School Orchestra Association, the American Symphony Orchestra League, Aspen Music School, the Association of Performing Arts Presenters, Interlochen Center for the Arts, and Tanglewood Music Center.

Opera Performer

Opera singers can find employment as opera choristers or solo artists. It is rare that an opera singer will find year-round employment from one company in North America. Only a few major opera companies offer year-round chorus contracts. Most companies offer per-performance contracts for solo roles and chorus positions. (Many of the smaller budgeted opera houses use a volunteer chorus.)

Because the majority of opera companies do not offer year-round contracts, opera singers tend to be transient—moving from one engagement to the next. Singers' fees vary drastically depending on the size of the role, the budget of the opera house, and the reputation of the artist. Transportation, housing, per diem, and other items may also be negotiated into the fee.

To build one's performance calendar and to become a more diversified artist, a singer's career may incorporate recital, chamber, and concert engagements, or other nonoperatic engagements. Also, North American singers will often include international engagements on their calendars.

Ideally, casting takes place after an artist has been seen in performance. However, auditioning is a large component of a singer's career. Most major opera companies travel to New York City at least once a year to hear auditions for future seasons. With few exceptions, companies hold house auditions for local and visiting artists. Companies tend to cast one to five years out, depending on the size of the company.

Most established singers have management to assist them in scheduling auditions, negotiating contracts, serving as liaison for other company relations, and building their careers. Artist managers also hold auditions annually, but often approach singers after seeing them in performance or competitions.

Once hired for an opera engagement, singers can expect music and staging rehearsals to run approximately two weeks, with an additional week for technical and dress rehearsals on stage. The average house presents three performances of each production over the course of one-and-a-half weeks; however, in larger houses or festivals, a production may run for a couple of months. In most cases, singers are responsible for learning the role prior to the first rehearsal.

A successful singer's career is balanced with performances, ongoing training of the eclectic skills required of a performing opera singer, and continual study of new repertoire. Singers must constantly be building their artistry with the assistance of their support network, which can include voice teacher, coach, artist manager, and other opera professionals.

The productive years for performing opera singers can be fewer than workers in other fields; therefore, singers must be savvy with finances. Upon retiring from performing, some singers look to teaching and administrative careers as alternative professions.

Skills and Preparation

Opera is a multidisciplinary art form that incorporates all the arts and, as such, requires performers to be skilled in many different areas. With the assistance of professionals across the field, OPERA America, the service organization for the field of opera, compiled a list of important skills and traits for the professional singer. This is not a definitive list; rather, it is a starting point. Singers should be in constant contact with their network for recommendations for additional skills.

- *vocal/musical skills:* solid vocal technique, vocal expressiveness, beautiful sound, individual artistry, ability to learn a score/basic musical skills, and use of vocal coloring
- *dramatic skills:* engaging stage persona, acting skills, versatility, ability to move well, dance skills, ability to take direction, role/text interpretation, Alexander technique, ability to research/study a character, and facial expression/focus
- *related skills/areas of knowledge:* languages (diction), languages (comprehension), knowledge of opera's traditions, piano skills, knowledge of related subjects (e.g., history, art)

- *business skills:* audition skills, goal-setting skills, networking skills, negotiating skills, writing skills, and financial skills
- *personal traits:* discipline, dependability, professional demeanor, collegial behavior, drive, perseverance, confidence, mental health, ability to live with rejection, ability to assess feedback, charisma, knowledge about one's own limitations, willingness to travel, ability to build and maintain relationships, intellectual curiosity, spiritual fortitude, ability to establish a realistic workload, and ability to identify problems rationally

Assessing talent and skills is an ongoing process, and honesty is imperative. Singers will greatly improve their chances of success if they listen carefully to advice given and are willing to change and grow.

In the early stages of their careers, singers can find training opportunities, which may pay minimal stipends. A few major opera houses have year-round training programs that are salaried positions. Most existing training programs are shorter in length (four weeks to nine months) with varying compensation.

There is no one clear path to success in the operatic performing realm. Throughout their training and career, singers must incorporate private study. In terms of formal education, many singers complete an undergraduate, graduate, and conservatory education. (A doctorate is not a requirement of the performing field, although it may be helpful in acquiring a faculty position following a performing career.)

Upon completion of a rigorous academic program, a singer often looks for a training program. These programs come in all shapes and sizes: some require a fee, some pay a stipend; some provide only outreach performance opportunities, some offer a balance of training and performance opportunities; some are only four weeks, some are year-round; some take place in Europe and some take place in North America; some are stand-alone training programs and some are sponsored by professional opera companies.

Young singers should carefully consider their own needs when exploring these programs. Once singers have assessed their needs, they can explore the options available. OPERA America's Singer Services program provides a variety of publications that can give a singer a clearer picture of programs and opportunities available. These tools should be used in tandem with the advice offered by the singer's support network (voice teacher, coach, etc.).

A young singer's experience often includes competitions, opera chorus experience, and leading and supporting roles with smaller opera companies. According to OPERA America's fifth edition of the *Career Guide for Singers,* there are more than eighty North American opera companies that sponsor training programs for young singers, approximately forty institutes and workshops for advanced singer training, eighty-five competitions for singers in North America, and an additional fifty competitions around the world from which North American singers can benefit.

Although the number of opera houses, training programs, and competitions is growing in North America, achieving a successful career is still a challenge. In the 2000 edition of *Musical America International Directory of the Performing Arts,* approximately 3,100 singers are listed as currently under management. The opera field is a competitive one, and successful singers must be blessed with a unique talent backed with training, experience, connections, perseverance, and an element of luck.

Compiled with the assistance of OPERA America and the Washington Opera.

Armed Forces Musician

The United States Army, Navy, Air Force, Marine Corps, and Coast Guard* each maintain a variety of performing ensembles and offer career opportunities for all types of musicians. Positions are available for both men and women as accompanists, arrangers, band and orchestra members, vocalists, conductors, music librarians, transcribers, pianists, recording technicians, instructors, and instrument-repair people. Military ensembles perform at military ceremonies, social events, public relations concerts, recruiting shows, and at music education and patriotic events. In any branch of the service, a musician can look forward to a career involving extensive travel and benefits that include a pay scale competitive with civilian wages, free medical care, commissary and post exchange privileges, and retirement pay. Even if a musician decides not to devote his or her entire career to military service, the training will be excellent preparation for a civilian music career.

Recruit Training and the Armed Forces School of Music
In the Army, Navy, and Marine Corps, recruits attend a twenty-three-week course at the Armed Forces School of Music in Norfolk, Virginia, after receiving basic (known also as "recruit") training. Air Force musicians and those in the other service branches who are slated for premier musical organizations do not attend the school. In addition, members of the United States Marine Band ("The President's Own") and The United States Coast Guard Band are exempt from recruit training—the only musicians in any branch of the armed forces to be so exempted.

---

*The Coast Guard is technically not part of the armed forces except in time of war.

Opportunities and Options for Military Musicians

Air Force: The United States Air Force Band (nicknamed "America's Band" and based in Washington, D.C.) and the United States Air Force Band of the Rockies (based in Colorado Springs) are the premier bands in the Air Force, which maintains a total of twelve bands throughout the U.S. and overseas. Because musicians who enlist in the Air Force do not attend the Armed Forces School of Music, they must possess high levels of musical skill before joining. Generally speaking, qualified applicants know to which band they will be assigned before enlisting in the Air Force.

Army: The Army is the largest branch of the military and maintains more than one hundred bands in the active and reserve forces in the continental United States and abroad. The premier bands are the U.S. Army Band ("Pershing's Own"), based in Washington, D.C.; the U.S. Army Field Band, which tours nationally and internationally; the U.S. Military Academy Band, which supports the corps of cadets at West Point; and the Old Guard Fife and Drum Corps, which performs Colonial-style music in Washington and around the world. Assignments to other Army bands can be guaranteed at the time of enlistment, ensuring an initial posting to the band of one's choice, as chosen from the list of vacancies.

Coast Guard: The United States Coast Guard maintains only one band, but like many other armed forces performing ensembles, it contains several subgroups, including woodwind and brass quintets, a swing band, and a Dixieland band.

Marine Corps: There are fourteen musical units in the U.S. Marine Corps. The United States Marine Band ("The President's Own") and the U.S. Marine Drum & Bugle Corps ("The Commandant's Own") are both premier bands and are based in Washington, D.C. There are also twelve other bands, located in the U.S. and overseas. "The Commandant's Own" is the only active-duty drum and bugle corps in the armed forces today. Recruits may submit their choices for assignment, and these assignments are honored whenever possible, based on the needs of the Marine Corps. Exceptionally well-qualified recruits are given a specific guarantee of assignment prior to enlistment.

Navy: The Navy has fourteen bands of varying sizes, each with other (smaller) performing groups attached. Of these bands, two are considered premier: The U.S. Navy Band (based in Washington, D.C.) and the U.S. Naval Academy Band (based in Annapolis, Maryland). Other than those assigned to these two bands, new recruits don't have a choice as to where they will serve. However, once they graduate from the School of Music, their desires are taken into consideration by the assignment detailer, and an effort is made to accommodate those desires.

Opportunities for Advancement
The premier bands of each of the armed forces audition only for specific vacancies. Positions in these bands are open to any qualified musician, so those in nonpremier groups can aspire to these positions, even if they do not start out there.

In addition, the Armed Forces School of Music offers intermediate-level training in pedagogy and arranging, as well as advanced training in conducting/band leading. Such further study is recommended for those seeking promotion to higher ranks.

Musicians in Time of Conflict
In time of conflict, bands continue to serve as musicians first and foremost, providing morale concerts to troops, though there is a possibility that Navy band members may be asked to man damage control stations at sea in case of attack.

In the Army, the primary mission of bands in a combat theater is to perform music, but they also have a secondary mission—to augment command post security and guard enemy prisoner-of-war compounds.

Marines may be called upon to augment base operations in the U.S. or to act as security detachments in a theater of war.

It is rare for premier band members to be deployed outside the U.S.

Skills and Preparation
Requirements and opportunities vary from branch to branch, but a high level of musical skill on one's instrument is essential, and, in all cases, auditions are held prior to enlistment. A solid working knowledge of

music is a prerequisite for employment in music organizations in all branches of the armed forces.

Before acceptance into military music programs, musicians must demonstrate working knowledge of major or minor scales and fundamentals of music notation and terminology. They must be able to sight-read first-chair parts of standard band literature that is easy to moderately difficult or the second- and third-chair parts of literature that is moderately difficult to difficult, while properly observing phrasing, dynamics, and interpretation.

For more information about each branch's opportunities and requirements, contact a local recruiter, or visit that service branch's band Web site.

Compiled with the assistance of the United States Army Band, United States Marine Corps Band, United States Navy Band, United States Air Force Band, and United States Coast Guard Band.

Conductor

Many performing organizations such as orchestras, bands, choruses, ballet companies, and opera theaters require the leadership and expertise of a conductor. Although competition for conducting positions with major performing companies is fierce, opportunities with smaller organizations, particularly community groups, are more plentiful. In addition, the expansion of services by organizations such as major orchestras has opened up a new field of secondary positions.

The chief conductor of an orchestra may direct from 30 to 80 percent of the subscription concerts and make a number of guest conducting appearances in other cities. If a conductor is the music director as well, he or she generally has full responsibility for artistic decisions in addition to conducting duties.

Conducting staffs of large professional orchestras also may include any of the following: resident conductor, principal guest conductor, and associate and assistant conductors whose primary responsibilities are often pops or youth concerts.

Conductors of many small professional orchestras include those who conduct community, college, and youth orchestras. They generally hold these posts in conjunction with other full- or part-time positions as college or school music teachers, as musicians with larger symphonies, or as independent music instructors. In many community symphonies, the music director also assumes managerial duties if there is no professional manager.

Skills and Preparation

Because the conductor must be a well-developed musician, substantial experience as a performer, particularly with ensembles and orchestras, is essential. (Youth, high school, and college orchestras offer early playing experiences.) College or conservatory music study, including choral and instrumental conducting and orchestration courses, as well as a solid background in music history and performance practices, is also a requirement. In college, an aspiring conductor should get as much experience as possible directing student ensembles. Score-reading ability and a well-developed ear are important. Keyboard facility, particularly orchestral reduction (playing music from an orchestral score) is useful.

Aspiring conductors should continually expose themselves to live and recorded performances of all types of music. They should know not only the symphonic repertoire but all forms of musical expression. Personality is important too; vitality and leadership ability should go hand in hand with fine musicianship.

A great deal of conducting experience can be gained by working with college or conservatory student ensembles, with small community orchestras on a volunteer basis, or with youth orchestras at one of more than three hundred summer music camps in the United States. From time to time, professional orchestras sponsor conductor competitions modeled after the prestigious European competitions.

As part of the Tanglewood Music Center's Fellowship Program, young conductors have a chance to broaden their conducting experience. Under the guidance of well-known conductors, participants work with the Center's orchestra and smaller ensembles. Young conductors are selected by audition during the winter preceding each session.

The Aspen Music Festival and School operates the American Academy of Conducting at Aspen (AAC). The heart of the Academy experience is the opportunity to work with a skilled orchestra of experienced musicians. The Aspen Music Festival offers both intermediate and advanced conducting classes and opportunities to perform with its student orchestra. Participants are chosen by audition.

Interlochen Arts Academy offers a full-year conducting course in which each student prepares music, conducts a lab ensemble, and receives immediate feedback from the instructor and other students. Prerequisites include a theory and musicianship class.

Compiled with the assistance of the American String Teachers Association with National School Orchestra Association, the American Symphony Orchestra League, Aspen Music School, the Association of Performing Arts Presenters, Interlochen Center for the Arts, and Tanglewood Music Center.

Orchestra Administrator

An important professional component of an orchestra is its management. Fund-raising, youth and adult educational activities, scheduling, public relations, marketing, financial planning and budgeting, artist contracts, and programming are among the manager's duties. The degree to which the manager personally handles these jobs depends on the organization's size, but he or she is ultimately responsible for the smooth functioning of all business aspects of the symphony orchestra. Many major orchestras maintain a full schedule for their musicians and have proportionately large administrative staffs (up to eighty people) to handle the many management aspects. Each orchestra has its own organizational style, and some staff positions may not exist in all parts of the country. The following descriptions of positions with major orchestra staffs are examples of administrative careers available:

The *Chief Executive Officer* (or President, Executive Director, General Manager, Managing Director, or Manager) is responsible to the orchestra's governing board for all aspects of operations, including implementation of board policies, long-range planning, contract and labor negotiations, coordination of fund-raising and ticket sales, and staff supervision. Salaries for CEOs of large orchestras are sometimes comparable to those paid to business executives in similar positions. To manage an orchestra, one must be knowledgeable about all aspects of orchestra operations: budgeting and finance, personnel relations, marketing, law, and music. One must combine administrative ability with a knowledge and love of the symphonic repertoire and an understanding of performance standards. Above all, an orchestra manager should be dedicated to the symphony orchestra field and to his or her own organization, and should be prepared for long days of attending concerts and openings, traveling with the orchestra, and additional responsibilities, such as conducting contract negotiations.

The *Assistant Manager* (or Operations Manager or Manager) assists with the management of orchestra operations, including the coordination of repertoire and guest artists and conductors and overseeing administrative personnel. Depending on the staff structure, the assistant manager may also be responsible for budgets and fiscal affairs, contracts and tour arrangements, and scheduling concerts.

The *Director of Development* is responsible for planning and executing annual fund-raising campaigns, preparing grant applications, and maintaining contribution records. The director of development serves as liaison between the board and fund-raising committees and may be in charge of developing endowment programs. A solid knowledge of budgeting, finance, marketing techniques, and direct mail and fund-raising psychology is essential for this job.

The *Director of Marketing and Public Relations* promotes events by writing and distributing news releases to the media, arranges for feature stories about the symphony, sets up press conferences and media coverage of all special symphony events, organizes the subscription campaign, and handles such jobs as designing brochures. Duties may also include preparing advertising copy as well as editing the program booklets, coordinating box office activities, handling ticket printing, developing sales reports, and supervising box office staff. (See also "Public Relations Specialist" on page 94.)

The *Director of Education* works with school teachers, volunteers, school administrators, and conductors to devise youth concerts and preparatory materials. The director frequently writes scripts; contracts mimes, dancers, and singers; creates activities that involve all members of the community with the orchestra; and produces adult educational programs such as preconcert lectures, recitals, and newsletters.

The *Business Manager* (or Controller or Bookkeeper) prepares budgets, financial statements, and reports and handles account payments, payroll, deposits, tax reports, and other financial matters.

The *Community Engagement* (or Outreach) *Director* is responsible for creating and managing a wide range of musical activities that help the orchestra reach wider and more diverse publics that do not normally frequent classical music concerts.

The *Librarian* maintains and distributes orchestra scores and parts, purchases or rents music, and enters bowings and other markings into the parts.

The *Personnel Manager* hires additional musicians as needed or finds substitutes; sees that musicians meet attendance, punctuality, and dress requirements; and ensures that management provides adequate facilities for the musicians. This position requires an individual who is fair-minded and diplomatic, one who has the respect of both musicians and administrators.

The *Stage Manager* sees that the stage is properly set and that backstage facilities are ready for rehearsals and performances.

Some orchestra positions do not fall within the administrative category and are often carried out by musicians in addition to their regular duties as performers. Clerical help may be part-time or volunteer. Smaller orchestras often pay only the manager on a full-time basis. Volunteers handle most of the administrative work in community orchestras.

Skills and Preparation

A good way to gain experience in orchestra management is by volunteering to work part-time or during the summer with a professional symphony orchestra. Few orchestras in the United States can afford to turn down a volunteer.

A creative volunteer can design an internship by deciding which aspect of orchestra administration is of interest and writing to the executive director. The director will then pass the internship proposal to the right person. Success is more likely if specifics are used as far as particular area of interest, rather than the statement that one is "willing to do anything for anyone."

A good start is to combine college music studies with business. Bachelor of Arts programs and graduate degrees in arts administration have been instituted at many colleges and universities. Harvard's Summer School Institute in Arts Management also offers a program of intensive study.

People who enter orchestra administration or management come from a wide range of educational backgrounds. Some have conservatory training; some majored in music performance, musicology, or music history in colleges or universities. These are all good preparation for a career in orchestra administration or management, but to get a good entry-level position, it helps to have some specific preparation.

The American Symphony Orchestra League's Orchestra Leadership Academy offers an excellent ten-day career preparation course, "Essentials of Orchestra Management." Recent college graduates, as well as orchestra employees in the very early stages of their careers, make up its student body. Write to the League's Director of Orchestra Leadership Academy, 33 West 60th Street, New York, NY 10023.

The Tanglewood Music Center in Boston has a program of volunteer internships for young candidates who are serious about arts administration. Through this summer program, interns act as the interface between the Boston Symphony's management organization and the public, and they get an overview of the operation of a major symphonic festival in the process.

Compiled with the assistance of the American String Teachers Association with National School Orchestra Association, the American Symphony Orchestra League, Aspen Music School, the Association of Performing Arts Presenters, Interlochen Center for the Arts, and Tanglewood Music Center.

Popular Music Musician

A tourist who asks a New York cab driver how to get to Carnegie Hall is told, "Practice, buddy, practice." The joke may be old, but the advice is sound.

If one's dream is a career in popular music, one must be aware that the field is extremely competitive. Even with talent, success depends on a great deal of hard work and an even greater degree of luck. Most performers who have made a name for themselves in popular music, when asked about how to get started, may say, "Don't." They will point out that no matter how glamorous life can be at the top, the road there gets pretty rocky and sometimes doesn't lead anywhere at all.

When asked, however, if they regret the struggle or would change their careers, the reply is invariably, "No." Many musicians, like artists in other fields, perform because they feel they must, because music is where their aptitude lies. They know their talent is above average; they believe they have something special to contribute or that they are good enough to make a living performing.

For those who feel that they were born to perform and are sure that they have a statement to make in popular music, the career possibilities are many. Rock, jazz, blues, country, folk, Latin, ethnic, and classical music mingle in a number of ways to create the sounds of today.

One can perform solo or as part of a group and can expect to play almost anywhere: at clubs, pubs, theaters, places of worship, schools, parks, fairs, and summer festivals. A performer might even find a job in a television or movie studio, working for a major record company, or performing on music videos.

And any instrument is a possibility: Piano, guitar, synthesizer, saxophone, trumpet, and drums fit into most musical ensembles, but a mark can be made with anything from a harmonica to a sitar. Often, an unusual combination of instruments gives performing groups a uniquely appealing sound. Mastering more than one instrument or singing as well as playing increases the chances for success.

To work in television, Los Angeles is the best bet; New York is no longer the largest outlet for televised music.

The recording industry in the United States is centered in Los Angeles, New York, and Nashville, but important work is being done in other cities, including Detroit, Chicago, and Atlanta. The center for professional musical theater is still New York, but theaters are sprouting up all over.

Most musicians working in television, theater, movies, or recording studios are session musicians, hired on a per-job basis. Some television shows have a permanent orchestra or band, but that is rare. Similarly, theaters and recording studios do not, as a rule, have house bands; when backup musicians are needed, they are drawn from a city's music community.

In any city, therefore, the same musicians turn up in any number of places. For example, a Chicago jazz trombonist leads a band in a neighborhood club on Monday nights, plays in someone else's combo on Wednesday, and backs a headliner in a supper club on weekends. While evenings are devoted to live performances, days might be spent in a recording studio cutting albums or recording radio commercials. That jazz trombonist is a successful professional musician, but does not do the same thing all the time. He or she survives in a tough profession by being good, versatile, reliable, and able to read virtually any piece of music.

Even after that important first break, things can be rough. Pay is minimal and bookings infrequent and uncertain. A second job is almost certainly a necessity. Finding work in music education is the best route to take; it not only allows the satisfaction of working in the music field, but may also provide performance opportunities. Performers should also consider a professional career in addition to music in order to have a strong alternative career if things do not work out. Even a job driving a cab or working in a restaurant will do on a temporary basis, as long as it provides adequate financial support and leaves time for music.

Skills and Preparation

If the big break does not come, it should not cause discouragement. There is a large number of unsung musicians who make a good, steady income doing what they love and know best: making music. It is generally from these ranks of hard-working musicians that "instant sensations" come.

To get started, one needs to establish a reputation—not with the general public, but among other musicians. That means going where other musicians work. Every sizable city has a music community, but larger cities obviously offer more contacts and opportunities. The city should be chosen based on the type of music one plays or one's ultimate career goals. Some cities are known for particular styles of music and provide unique training grounds for young musicians interested in that style. Nashville is the mecca for country and western musicians; Chicago gave birth to urban blues and is still one place to see masters of the genre in action; but Boston also has blues and Seattle also has country music. It is smart to first take advantage of what is available close to home, learn as much as possible, then move on. Experience is the key to success in this field.

To do any kind of studio work, one must be an excellent musician. There is simply no time for practice at home before a session. Studio musicians must be first-rate readers and extremely flexible. A saxophone player might have to play a musical comedy score in the morning and switch to a big band sound in the afternoon or have a record date for a country music album.

The ability to read music and the technical mastery of one's instrument are minimum requirements for a performing career. To develop skills, a performer should take full advantage of all the opportunities offered in school and in the community, such as playing in marching, concert, and dance bands; jazz and classical ensembles; orchestras; and school and church choirs. The aspiring musician might start a vocal or instrumental group and donate services to local functions such as club

48

meetings, dinners, Parent/Teacher Association meetings, church picnics, school dances, or private parties as a way to gain experience in performing. The organizational and performing experience will be invaluable.

A college degree, if at all possible, is a great help. The music theory and instrumental techniques taught in college give a solid foundation on which to build a performing repertoire.

Above all, performers must practice! Musicians, like athletes, can only keep their working muscles in shape through constant exercise. To be a successful performing musician, one must be in top form at all times.

Classical training in form, analysis, theory, and composition are important to the popular musician; harmonic knowledge and familiarity with classical technique will broaden any musician's musical horizon. That's especially true today when so many popular composers borrow from other musical idioms in search of fresh sound combinations.

As basic and essential as technical skills are for a musician or entertainer, it is individual style that will make a performer stand out. A singer, for example, is judged on voice and training, but never those qualities alone. Intensity, sincerity, warmth, stage personality, and a special, personal way of bringing life to lyrics are what make audiences sit up and take notice. One way to develop a personal style is to learn everyone else's style to find out what has not been done.

A musician can pick up technical skills in the classroom, but personal style can only be developed in front of an audience. A performer needs audience reaction to know if he or she is on the right track. Most cities have small clubs that specialize in certain kinds of music. It is important for a new performer to find the club that features his or her kind of music and get acquainted with the musicians.

One of the best ways for instrumentalists to break into the field is to find people who do the same thing; a trumpet player should know every other trumpet player in town. Getting to know other musicians and being accepted is necessary. Going to clubs and other performing spots and waiting for a chance to sit in on a session is the best way for a performer to get experience. That involves finding out which places hold amateur nights and taking advantage of all chances to perform in front of an audience. A performing musician should play as much as possible and practice the rest of the time. That can include studying and playing along with recordings of favorite artists to learn their techniques.

Until one is able to afford an agent or manager, one will have to find one's own bookings. It is wise to build a press kit as soon as possible including personal information, photographs, and press clippings. A performance tape might also be helpful in getting a job.

When a performer starts getting bookings, he or she may want to find an agent or manager. Performers will be spending a great deal of time improving old material and working on new acts and will not have the time for financial, legal, and public-relations work. The performer should also be familiar, however, with the business aspects of performing even if someone else handles these things.

Life as a performer will require long hours, travel, and tough competition. But the opportunities for a successful career do exist if one is willing to work. Believing strongly in oneself and having a mature, realistic awareness of one's options are the best ingredients to being one of the lucky ones.

Compiled with the assistance of the American Society of Composers, Authors, and Publishers (ASCAP), Broadcast Music, Inc. (BMI), and the International Association of Jazz Educators.

Composer/Arranger

Because of the wide range of specialties that exist, career opportunities for composers and arrangers are numerous. One's expertise and passion should be his or her guide to a specific area of focus, but a good composer can branch out into several areas over the course of a career.

There are a multitude of music publishers who seek new music to add to their catalogs. Most publishers require that, along with a score, composers submit a high-quality recording of a performance of their work. For this reason, it is important for composers to maintain close ties with fellow musicians.

Many organizations, ensembles, and individuals commission works—that is, they pay a composer to write a piece of music specifically for them. Sometimes, the composer has the freedom to do as he or she chooses in the composition. In other cases, the commissioner has something specific in mind, and the composer's composition must meet certain requirements.

Composers often serve residencies, which means that they are supported financially while they spend a certain period of time in a community or with a music organization or institution. Such an experience is beneficial for both the composer and the others involved. Information about residencies—as well as information about competitions, professional development, and career opportunities—is available from the American Composers Forum, the national service organization for composers.

Television, the recording arts, and film are very high-profile areas that one may want to try to break into, although that road could be a

Music Business

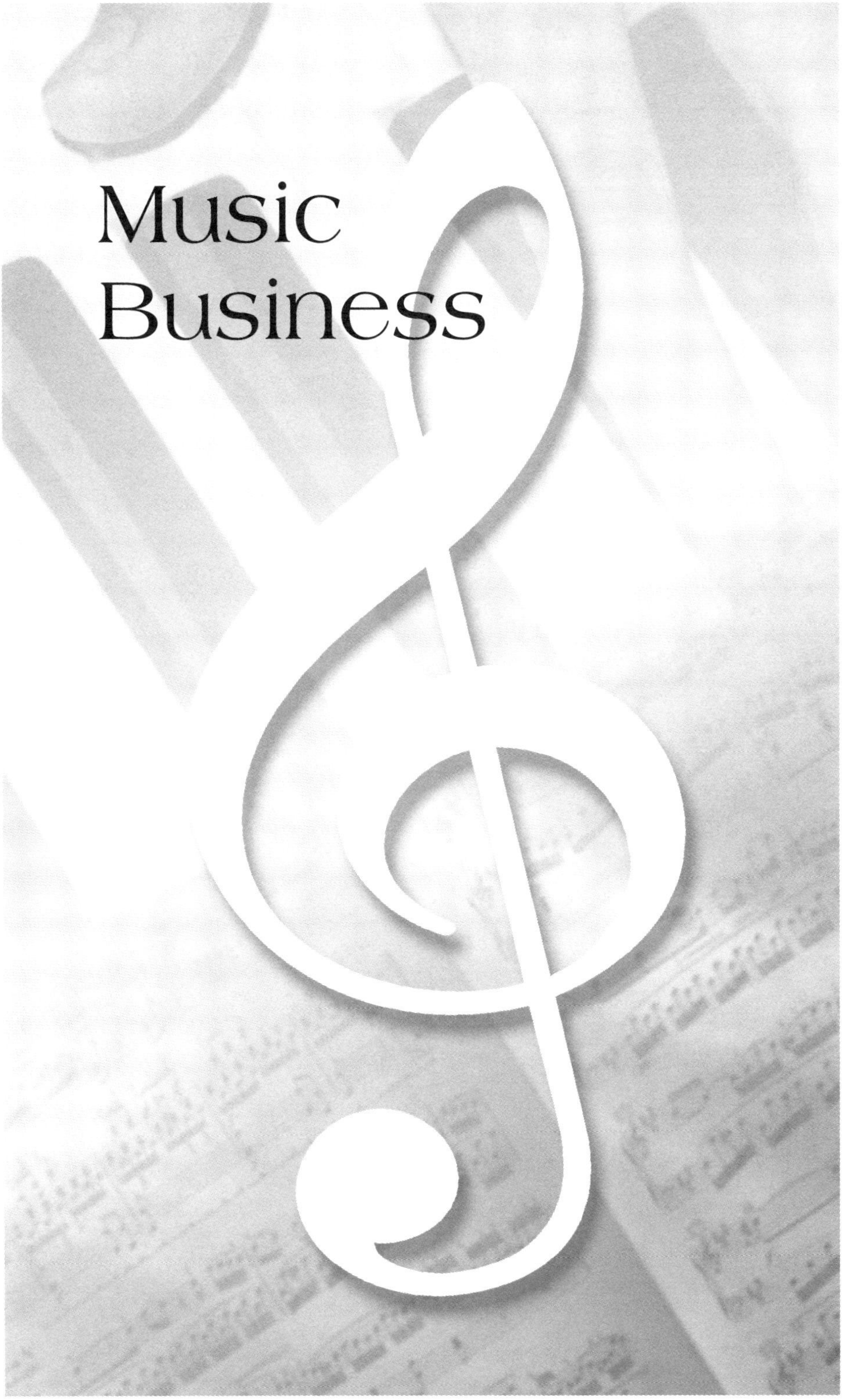

From the supply and maintenance of instruments to the publication of music scores, millions of individuals with a knowledge of music provide important services to amateur and professional musicians. Options within the field of music business are many. In the career you choose, you may or may not work directly with the public. The work that you decide to pursue may require a broad education including both business and music study, or it may require apprentice-like training with an experienced instrument maker. There are numerous variables to consider. This chapter will give you an overview of the many types of business-related music careers that are available.

Retailer

If one plays a musical instrument, it more than likely came from one of the thousands of retail stores that employ people in every capacity from *manager* to *teacher* to *instrument repair specialist.* While there are retail chains with music stores in several states, most owners operate just one or two stores and get involved in every aspect of their business.

There are four main types of music retailers:
- the full-line dealer who carries all types of instruments and musical accessories
- the school music dealer who specializes in band and orchestra instruments and amplification equipment
- the keyboard dealer who concentrates on pianos, organs, synthesizers, and electronic keyboards, and generally travels from school to school calling on educators
- the combo/sound reinforcement dealer who sells primarily amplifiers, guitars, electronic keyboards, and synthesizers

While the majority of musical instruments and accessories are sold through music retailers, some instruments, such as portable keyboards, are also sold by department stores and mass merchandisers. A variety of sound reinforcement equipment is also available through audio stores.

Many large music stores have extensive studio teaching operations, requiring in-store space, often managed by an *educational director* who is an authority in the music education field. In many cases, the educational director is also the store's contact with music teachers in private studios, public and parochial elementary and secondary schools, area colleges, and conservatories. This person is usually the primary teacher at the store.

The educational director arranges store recitals, oversees educational operations, and often leads workshops for music teachers. In addition to teaching, the director may also initiate in-school, group-instruction programs (working with local faculty members); arrange band and orchestra competitions; work with community band programs; and engage in public relations efforts that promote store sales.

In a large full-line music store, there are managers for each department who supervise sales personnel and take part in the general operation of the store. *Sales managers* usually rise from the ranks of sales personnel after proving their abilities. Age and seniority are not the only criteria for advancement. Extensive knowledge of a particular product area (such as guitars and amplifiers) can help a young person advance more quickly to a supervisory post. Sales managers also order merchandise, evaluate inventory and turnover, and set performance standards and sales quotas for all personnel.

In medium- and large-sized music retail outlets, other management opportunities may include being a department or division manager, such as in the sheet music, repair and service, shipping, accessories, or instrument rental department.

Annual salaries for music store salespeople vary depending upon ability and motivation and the reputation of the particular store. Store location, brands of instruments the store carries, and the promotion, advertising, and public relations support by the store owner and manufacturer also influence the earnings of the sales staff.

Many pay plans are available, including straight commission, combined salary and commission, or straight salary. (For current information about salary and types of payment, contact NAMM: International Music Products Association in Carlsbad, California, for a copy of its Compensation and Benefits Study.)

Skills and Preparation
Regardless of a retailer's specialty (such as providing a teaching stu-dio) or the depth of music it provides, the basic skill required in retail-

ing is the ability to sell. With increasing new technology, product knowledge is also extremely important, especially in combo instrument sales.

Anyone with a gift for persuasion and sense of conviction can sell. But in a music store, the ability to play an instrument is very helpful in counseling the customer.

And, because retailing is becoming increasingly complex, more and more music store managers also want employees with college degrees. Many colleges/universities now offer a combined music/business degree program for musically oriented people who want to pursue nonperformance careers; write to NAMM for a list of these (NAMM also offers scholarships through these schools).

Computer knowledge is also a big plus in music retailing because many stores run the inventory on computer and on a Web site and may even sell through e-commerce.

Also, many larger music retail stores (usually those in the full-line category) offer internships or work-study programs for students enrolled in joint-degree programs at area colleges and universities. Smaller retailers may have entry-level openings for students without college training who have a deep interest and performing proficiency in music. The possibilities for advancement to a management position without a college degree, especially if there is competition from employees with business administration courses or degrees, are slim. Those who cannot afford to attend college full-time should consider evening courses in business and retailing.

Many music retailers looking for college-trained employees rely on recommendations from music educators at area colleges and universities. Top managers of large, multistore operations often recruit on college campuses across the country for their beginning management and sales personnel. If, however, one is not a college-trained person but has an interest in music and sales, one can usually explore job opportunities by establishing personal contact with local music retailers.

In the large music stores, the in-store educational director usually has at least a bachelor's degree in music education (preferably a master's degree) and teaching experience. This background makes the director the professional equal of the teachers who are customers and tends to attract these people to the store.

Retailers who operate more than one outlet usually choose outstanding sales managers to run the individual stores. Again, the criteria for advancement to store manager are administrative and sales ability and solid background and experience in the business skills needed to run a retail store for maximum profit.

NAMM offers more than three hundred books and products focused on helping music products retailers run better businesses. Through NAMM University, there are more than thirty different courses offered around the country and online, in the areas of sales, management, financial management, merchandising, promotions, small business skills and rep skills, among other topics. NAMM University products and courses are listed on their Web site (www.namm.com) or by contacting them directly.

After working in music sales, one may eventually want to open a music store. The person who establishes a retail store generally has experience selling musical instruments, accessories, and supplies. A store owner should be well trained in business administration, merchandising, advertising and promotion, sales, and personnel management. Most successful music retailers have risen through the ranks and have combined a college degree in business or music with an inherent love of music and practical selling experience.

The following are the major requisites for a successful music store owner:
- sufficient capital backing and source of financing
- good store location in the right market
- business acumen, sensitivity to people, and solid educational background in business administration and music
- administrative ability and management skills
- demonstrated salesmanship
- ability to play an instrument and interest in music performance
- interest in music education; knowing the latest trends at all levels of school music instruction, as well as teaching approaches and programs of major manufacturers and manufacturers' associations

- good personal and professional relationships and rapport with independent and group teachers, school music personnel, and college music faculty members, as well as church and civic personnel
- strong sense of public and community relations and true involvement in the community

Successful music retailers never really stop selling, even when they can afford to hire all the sales personnel they need. They stay active in professional associations, educator groups, and civic and business organizations at the local, state, and national levels.

Compiled with the assistance of NAMM: International Music Products Association.

Band Instrument Service and Repair Technician

Technicians in the field of band instrument repair clean, adjust, remove dents, solder, install new pads and corks, and work on myriad mechanical parts and mechanisms on clarinets, flutes, saxophones, oboes, bassoons, cornets, trumpets, trombones, baritones, French horns, tubas, and sousaphones. Although the trend is leaning toward "playing condition repairs," many shops still overhaul (i.e., make like new, refinish) older instruments. Most technicians play-test the instruments when the repairs are completed, but this does not mean technicians have to fully master each instrument to be qualified.

Most technicians are considered "general practitioners" because they work on all makes and models of woodwind, brasswind, and percussion products. About 20 to 25 percent of these general practitioners also work on stringed instruments. Some technicians specialize in specific areas or types of horns such as woodwind or brass instruments only. Because many of the repair techniques are similar for each, a technician should learn as much as possible when entering the trade before deciding to specialize.

Band instrument repair technicians are usually associated with a retail music store. Most repair shops are located within the store, but it is not uncommon for them to be located off site. A growing number of technicians are considered independents and work for themselves, usually out of their homes. A very small number of technicians work for manufacturers of band instruments.

There is a shortage of competent band instrument repair technicians today. Many of the older technicians are retiring and too few young

Piano Tuner

A piano tuner/technician tunes the piano, regulates the mechanism to optimum performance, and makes necessary repairs to or replacements of parts. Most of the work is done in people's homes, where most pianos are located. Tuner/technicians also work in schools, conservatories, studios, places of worship, concert halls, music stores, and piano rebuilding shops.

Most piano tuner/technicians are independent, relying on their reputations for business and developing a clientele over a period of years. Some, however, work as regular employees of or on contract with schools and music stores.

Besides learning the skills involved in becoming proficient, an independent piano tuner/technician must be personable and capable of personal and business discipline to be successful.

Piano tuner/technicians frequently specialize in particular kinds of work. Such specialties might concentrate on keyboard repair, concert and studio piano maintenance (usually possible only in metropolitan areas), or restoration of antique instruments. Not all of these specialties require the ability to tune.

Some larger public school systems and many universities and colleges have piano tuner/technicians as full-time staff members and provide shop space, tools, materials, regular hours, and fringe benefits. Because these positions offer almost automatic prestige and security not so easily achieved in independent practice, salaries may be somewhat lower than a well-established independent piano tuner would earn. However, because of the requirements of music school faculties, standards for these positions are usually quite high.

In certain areas of the country, music stores may pay a salary and possibly a commission to piano tuner/technicians for doing in-home service for customers. In these situations, the store handles the management functions of taking calls, arranging appointments, and collecting fees from customers. Employed tuner/technicians may enjoy an assured income and fringe benefits they would otherwise have to provide for themselves, but standards of performance and potential earnings are then dictated by the employer.

The personal freedom and independence possible for well-trained piano tuner/technicians, combined with the near-professional relationship that they have with clients and the satisfaction they get from combining intellect and hand to recreate beauty, attracts many young men and women to the field. While job success depends on many factors, the fact remains that as long as there are pianos, piano tuner/technicians will be needed.

Piano tuner/technicians are not regulated or licensed. Voluntary associations are active, however, in establishing standards of professional competence and conduct. The Piano Technicians Guild, for example, offers examinations and certification.

Skills and Preparation

Tuning is an acquired skill not at all related to musical talent or ability to identify pitches. First, a tuner's ear must be trained to hear the interference (called beats) caused by two nearly identical frequencies of sound. Also, a tuner's mind must be trained to know how to use the speed of beats to establish "equal temperament," usually on a pitch source of standard frequency, such as a tuning fork or an electronic device. Finally, a tuner must develop coordination between the ear and hand, manipulating the tuning lever to accomplish minute adjustments of tension in each of a piano's 225-odd strings.

Learning this process and becoming proficient takes time and practice. Some electronic devices can aid in learning and practice but are not a substitute for the judgment required of the trained ear in dealing with pianos having varying degrees of inharmonicity.

While the theory of tuning can be learned through a correspondence course or a book, a significant amount of personal instruction interspersed with practice is needed to achieve the right results. Generally, a piano tuner's training must include work on at least one thousand pianos. Working in a music store is an excellent way to develop proficiency and gain experience before starting an independent practice.

The typical piano tuner of years ago usually had only enough knowledge of piano mechanics to make silent notes play or to patch broken parts. In contrast, today's piano tuner/technician learns to fine-regulate the piano action and keys to factory specifications with a variety of special tools.

Broken or malfunctioning parts on newer pianos can usually be taken care of through replacement and reregulation. Sometimes replacement parts are not readily available because of the age of the piano; in that case, a tuner should be able to make or adapt parts that will function correctly. Both the piano student and the accomplished musician have a right to expect that their tuner/technician maintain instruments at optimum levels of mechanical and musical performance.

Compiled with the assistance of the National Piano Foundation, Piano Manufacturers Association International, and the Piano Technicians Guild.

Distributor

For the business-minded person who likes selling but does not want to go into retailing, distribution offers another challenging career possibility.

The distributor, the liaison between manufacturer and retailer, buys and warehouses many types of instruments, sheet music, and accessories and resells them to music retailers large and small. The distributor also imports instruments in quantities large enough to make them competitively priced for consumer resale.

Most distributors assign *salespeople* to specific territories, which might encompass several states. Salespeople provide advice to retailers on best-selling products and merchandising techniques, displaying new products, and taking orders.

Some distributors also *manufacture* small instruments in their own facilities or may be the exclusive importers of instruments manufactured abroad to their own specifications and under their own names. (See "Instrument Manufacturer/Maker," p. 71.)

In addition, opportunities exist in the distribution area for *advertising specialists,* including *artists* and *copy writers.* Many distributors also have their own repair and maintenance service staff as well as personnel in charge of stock, packing and shipping, and taking orders. (See "Band Instrument Service and Repair Technician," p. 63.)

Skills and Preparation
Educational requirements for jobs in the field of music distribution vary. The distribution manager should have a business background in

addition to an appreciation of music. Distribution managers should be able to work well with others, know the capabilities and limitations of the products being sold, and have management and leadership skills.

Compiled with the assistance of the International Association of Electronic Keyboard Manufacturers, the Music Distributor Association, and the National Association of Band Instrument Manufacturers.

Instrument Manufacturer/ Maker

Job opportunities in instrument manufacturing have grown over the years as increased interest in making music has swelled the ranks of both amateur and professional musicians. The resulting demand for all types of instruments and accessories has fueled the growth of many manufacturers and encouraged the development of many new products and new processes for efficient production. Computers and electronic circuitry are an integral part of many of the new products and the equipment and processes used to make them.

For centuries, the production of musical instruments was the work of skilled artisans who carefully handcrafted and assembled the various pieces. Some of the handcrafting aspects of manufacturing have been changed by technological advances. Assembly line methods and new materials and technologies, such as plastics and electronics, have greatly affected the industry.

The design and manufacture of synthesizers and electronic instruments, along with the computer-controlled machinery used to produce them, requires the talents of *engineers* and *programmers* who understand microcircuitry and computer technology. Because electronic instruments contain chips to handle a variety of functions, engineers must understand not only the functions of the components but their musical potential as well.

Different skills are required for the manufacture of various instruments. There is a need in all phases, however, for *tool and die makers, assemblers, screw machine operators, buffers, sanders, tuners,* and *quality assurance technicians.* Manufacturers of brass and some woodwind instruments have positions for *die casters, solderers, engravers, lacquerers, platers, valve makers,* and others skilled in assembling various elements as the instruments near completion.

There are few shortcuts in the manufacture of quality pianos, guitars, violins, and other stringed instruments. (A maker of stringed instruments is called a luthier.) Modern production methods may be used to manufacture metal interior pieces and for primary woodworking, veneering, and mill operations (for example, the use of numeric milling machines is becoming widespread), but the final product is the result of handcrafting and skilled artisanship.

Among traditional musical instruments, drums have perhaps benefited most from the development of new materials. Plastics have replaced animal skins as drumheads and are widely used for the bodies. The finished drum, however, still requires handwork. Skilled craftsmanship is necessary for gluing joints, centering the head, trimming, sanding, and tuning. The final assembly of any instrument, in fact, is reserved for the best-trained and most highly-skilled members of the production staff.

After completion, each instrument is evaluated by a quality assurance technician before it leaves the plant. Quality assurance technicians must be musicians as well as craftsmen, familiar with the instrument and its musical capabilities, and able to make minor adjustments or pinpoint problems for adjustment by others on the production line.

Another possibility for a career in instrument manufacturing lies in design and development—one could be an *inventor.* Often, specialists in other fields, such as electronics and engineering, computer software, or music performance, have invented new instruments that have led to the development of new industries.

Influential musical instrument inventors have included John Philip Sousa, sousaphone; Laurens Hammond, electric organ; Harold Rhodes, electric piano; Robert Moog and RCA engineers Harry Olson and Herbert Belar, synthesizer; and John Chowning of Stanford University, digital synthesizer. Hundreds of others have made refinements to basic instruments or created accessory items, amplification equipment, and adapters that have broadened the capabilities of instruments or made them easier to play.

Skills and Preparation

Job opportunities for a career in musical instrument manufacturing are available all across the United States. The only basic skill necessary for a beginning job is the ability to learn, because most manufacturers have on-the-job training programs. Some firms also have apprenticeship programs for the more skilled craft positions.

In addition, while some production functions can be handled by a person without musical training, knowing how to play the instrument being manufactured is an important asset. According to one manufacturer, knowing how to play an instrument might be compared to having a college degree in another field. In many instances a college degree helps to progress to a more skilled, better-paying job.

In most organizations, production management personnel are recruited from the ranks of experienced and skilled production staff. Management-level personnel can often, however, move to other companies in the industry or even to management jobs in completely different fields.

Compiled with the assistance of the Guitar and Accessories Marketing Association, the International Association of Electric Keyboard Manufacturers, the Music Industry Conference, the National Association of Band Instrument Manufacturers, the National Piano Foundation, and Piano Manufacturers Association International.

Other Manufacturing Personnel

Sales support personnel are important to manufacturing operations. Among these are *product specialists* who know and understand their particular product very well. Product specialists assist sales managers in demonstrations, educate salespeople and music retailers, and study the field directly related to the products for which they are responsible. They monitor and become the resident experts on all competitive products. These specialists usually are divided into groups: fretted instrument, woodwind, brass, keyboard, and percussion specialists.

Artist relations is an area that also can be very stimulating. *Artist relations specialists* are people who work with professional musicians to explore ideas for new musical products. They also recruit well-known professionals to represent the manufacturer in advertisements.

Especially important to a manufacturing plant is the service department, staffed by experts thoroughly familiar with the product. The *service staff* handles any problems with the product, gives advice and instruction, and sends replacement parts to clients when needed.

Skills and Preparation
Instrument manufacturer employees who work directly with the public should have excellent communication skills. In addition, product specialists should have excellent product knowledge, be organized and detail oriented, be able to create and design training material, and have excellent teaching skills. The artist relations specialist should have previous experience with artists, specifically with tours, trade shows,

and demonstrations. The service staff should have technical knowledge specifically related to the product and be computer literate.

Compiled with the assistance of the Guitar and Accessories Marketing Association, the International Association of Electric Keyboard Manufacturers, the Music Industry Conference, the National Association of Band Instrument Manufacturers, the National Piano Foundation, and Piano Manufacturers Association International.

Sales Representative

Most manufacturers have a field organization of sales representatives who are strategically located throughout the country and are responsible for particular territories. Some companies use the services of manufacturers' representatives who handle several brand names.

As direct-to-retail sales by manufacturers becomes more commonplace, there is a corresponding need for a trained staff of *telemarketers* in addition to field sales representatives. Telemarketing representatives who have a knowledge of music tend to be the best representatives because they speak the language of the storekeeper and his or her staff and are usually successful in conveying to the potential customer the merits of various products.

Sales representatives may report to a regional field representative, but they often work directly with the company *sales manager* who is located at or near company headquarters. The sales manager, using product and market studies and statistics developed from company and industry experience as well as outside mercantile information, must project instrument requirements for months ahead to be used as a production guide.

Overall, the sales manager plans and carries out all company sales meetings, hires and trains sales representatives, arranges and sometimes attends dealer meetings, and takes care of all details related to the sales staff.

Sales representatives and sales managers work for many different businesses within the music industry, including publishers and record companies, as well as manufacturers and distributors. (See also "Distributor," p. 69, and "Instrument Manufacturer/Maker," p. 71.)

Skills and Preparation

Successful sales representatives must know their product and establish good business relations with clients in their area. A college degree in business is helpful but not necessary. An up-to-the-minute familiarity with the market and competitive conditions is also mandatory. A sales representative must be a self-starter, dependable, and able to communicate, but need not play an instrument.

Compiled with the assistance of the Guitar and Accessories Marketing Association, the International Association of Electric Keyboard Manufacturers, the Music Industry Conference, NAMM: International Music Products Association, the National Association of Band Instrument Manufacturers, the National Piano Foundation, and Piano Manufacturers Association International.

Music Publisher

Music publishing is a multifaceted field made up of interdependent operations, each involving specific career opportunities. The publishing process begins with the selection of the music to be published, whether it is an original composition, a method, or a new arrangement of an existing piece.

In some firms, the selection of pieces to be published is handled by the *director of publications,* who may also serve as an *editor.* The qualifications for this position almost defy description because the work calls for highly developed musical taste, a strong sense of the market, and an eye on the budget.

Sometimes the director of publications accepts, rejects, or commissions a work; sometimes the decision is made by a committee. In other instances, it is made by the head of the music publishing company.

Once a work is accepted for publication, it must be readied for production. An editor reviews the manuscript and makes sure that everything is in perfect order, from the proper spelling of the title to the last dynamic mark on the page.

When the editor finishes, the manuscript is processed into a form suitable for printing. At one time, most printed music was engraved by hand by etching the music out of a soft metal plate with special tools. More recently, music typewriters, autography, and dry transfers of preprinted self-adhering notes and symbols were used. Now, computer programs are used by *notesetters* to produce output either as printed pages or as digital files.

The processed pages must then be proofread. Both the composer and a professional proofreader make sure that the music to be printed conforms to the manuscript.

The work is returned to the notesetter, who makes the necessary changes, and then it is given a final check by the proofreader.

With the music completed, an *artist* designs the cover and adds any necessary sketches or photos. The work is then ready for final printing.

After the composition is printed, the next step is to let the public know about it. This is the responsibility of *advertising professionals* (see "Marketing Specialist/Advertiser" on p. 76), who need special training. While the career opportunities for advertising professionals are similar throughout the music publishing field, there are a number of areas in which the professionals can specialize, including the following:

- *standard publishing* of master works, special editions, and publication of past and present serious music
- *educational publishing,* concentrating on both instructional and performance material for preschool to college levels
- *popular music publishing,* revolving around current songs and standards (songs that maintain their popularity after their initial success)

Further career opportunities exist in music promotion. Some companies specializing in music for school use lecturers and clinicians to maintain contact with educators who are potential customers.

Companies that publish concert music, ballets, and operas naturally try to encourage the performance of such works. Some large publishers with extensive catalogs in these areas maintain a promotion staff, which may include several full-time employees. These people bring the publisher's repertoire to the attention of performing organizations and individual performers through personal contact and written materials such as catalogs, press releases, and newsletters. Smaller companies may assign promotion of such works to a staff member who also has other responsibilities within the company.

In addition to promotion people, publishers with catalogs of symphonic and operatic music maintain rental libraries to furnish materials for works that are not available for sale. A *rental librarian* must have a good working knowledge of the requirements of orchestras and other performing groups, as well as the ability to ensure accurate deliveries while working under deadline pressure.

In popular music publishing, a key role is played by the *creative manager,* whose responsibilities vary from company to company. Generally, however, creative managers are in charge of acquiring new songs, securing recording contracts for the writer-artist, and arranging for the recording of the music.

Large popular music publishers have a staff of promotion personnel, while smaller companies may hire outside promotion specialists to promote individual recordings of works that they publish.

Although most publishing firms employ outside counsel for complex legal issues, there is a need for a *copyright department manager,* an in-house employee with a good working knowledge of copyright procedures and their implications for the music publishing business. Much of this knowledge can be obtained through on-the-job training and familiarity with copyright law, the procedures of the United States Copyright Office, protection of rights throughout the world, and other aspects of copyright.

Closely identified with the copyright department manager (and frequently the same person) is the *rights and permissions manager.* This job involves the licensing of copyrights of the company's music for use in recordings, movies, television films, commercials, etc., and arrangements for publication by others.

All types of music publishers also require good *accounting and bookkeeping personnel.* In addition to the normal accounting and record-keeping requirements of any business (accounts receivable and payable, maintenance of a general ledger, and tax preparation and filing), music publishers are responsible for the payment of royalties to composers and lyricists for sales, rentals, recordings, and all other uses of the works they represent. A music background is not essential, but a good music publishing accountant or data processor must be comfortable working in a business in which most of the activity is made up of small transactions, all of which must be properly accounted for down to the smallest detail.

Skills and Preparation
While there are music publishing companies scattered around the country, the centers for the business have traditionally been the New York metropolitan area, Los Angeles, and Nashville.

Composers, music editors, and proofreaders generally have similar backgrounds. Although a composer's area of expertise may vary from the editor's or proofreader's, all should have as broad a background as possible in all areas of music. An understanding of the composition and arranging processes, music notation, style, and form related to all types of music is a must.

Although many editors specialize, the broader one's base of knowledge the better; the opportunities are much greater for those who are well versed in all musical styles. There are, however, situations that call for a specialist with extensive general background coupled with a specific area of expertise (for example, keyboard music of the Baroque era). It would be advantageous for an editor, composer, or arranger who wants to specialize to acquire a solid general background before concentrating on a specific area.

For those who prefer the business side of publishing, the National Association of Recording Arts and Sciences (NARAS) Institute maintains a file on music business courses including those on copyright.

For anyone interested in becoming a notesetter, a thorough understanding of music is necessary. Many notesetters train themselves to use music notation computer software.

Advances in technology change the world of publishing every day. It is now possible to acquire printed music from a CD-ROM or the Internet. Therefore, it is recommended that those interested in entering the music publishing industry have a knowledge of computers and current technology.

If one were knowledgeable in all areas of music publishing, could one do everything oneself? Well, that's how many people begin. An individual with a love of music and its presentation in printed form is the potential future publisher. This type of person is often a specialist and has a point of view that he or she wants to convey to others. He or she starts by publishing in this field, performing all the functions previously discussed. As the business expands, others are hired and trained to handle specific functions in the overall production. It is easy to see, therefore, that some business background is also very important.

Compiled with the assistance of the Music Publishers Association and the National Music Publishers Association.

Music
Communications

Through the media, music communications professionals provide information about music and musicians to the public. Music communications professionals usually have a love of language and research in addition to their passion for music. The Internet has greatly expanded the amount and variety of published information about music, and e-mail has made telecommuting an increasingly viable option. There are many exciting opportunities in this ever-changing field.

Music Critic

A music critic's purpose is not simply to give a report card to performing musicians but to make a meaningful contribution to the art that nurtures them. At the same time, music critics are helping to expand the active audience by writing about music in a way that portrays it as a vital and stimulating experience. A critic's ideas can help expand the repertoire of the performer, concertgoer, and record collector. Critics do (or ought to do) research when they prepare to write about a major performance or recording, and that research may add substantially to their audience's general knowledge and understanding of a given work, composer, or entire period in music history.

Specific duties of music critics vary from one publication to another, depending on the size of its staff and the community it serves. A large metropolitan newspaper may have an actual staff of music specialists assigned to opera, early music, experimental music, and so on, as well as critics who review recordings but not live events. At smaller newspapers, a single critic may cover not only all musical events but drama, dance, films, and other arts as well. In addition to actual reviewing, most critics will do advances (feature stories before an artist's or organization's appearance in the area), and some will have the chance to express observations and opinions about music through a Sunday (essay-type) column. The Sunday column is also a place to talk about major developments of interest. The opportunity to write an occasional significant news story (an obituary, a piece on the appointment of a major new conductor, etc.) may also arise.

Even the most successful critics cannot expect financial rewards like those realized by people making similar commitments in other professions. One of the benefits of the profession is the opportunity to travel and report on premieres and festivals in other cities and countries. Few publications, however, have budgets to support such assignments; more often, it is the industrious freelancer, with arrangements to supply several different publications with reports on the same event, who does the traveling.

All music critics, paid or unpaid, do share one benefit: they can enjoy a feeling of considerable fulfillment, not in terms of being recognized in a restaurant or having reviews quoted, but in helping inform and stimulate their readers, both musicians and laypeople.

Skills and Preparation

Criticism should begin with a basic understanding between the critic and the person subject to criticism; they should speak the same language. In line with that, all music critics need musical training. Often, the hiring of music critics is slanted toward writers who know something about music rather than toward musicians who know something about writing. Most respected critics agree that critics need to be knowledgeable musicians capable of expressing themselves, rather than merely skilled wordsmiths with a smattering of musical knowledge.

The Music Critics Association of North America offers this list of requirements for the aspiring critic:

- a knowledge of the musical material being reviewed or written about, gained through education in an instrument or the study of music history or musicology; extensive listening experience is also essential
- a general knowledge of the arts, history, and the world at large
- a good ear—good genetically but also trained and tuned
- the ability to write clearly and focused toward the readership of a specific publication
- constant listening and writing
- the ability to identify personal preferences and dislikes and to separate them from objective judgment making
- involvement—a love for things musical, a high degree of enthusiasm, and even an idealism that communicates itself to the reader
- the willingness to stand up for a justifiable opinion that is supported by knowledge, fairness, and experience

In short, critics need a passion for music, the drive to communicate that passion, and the skill to make themselves understood. At the same time, they need the self-discipline to be dispassionate in their judgments. Ideally, a music critic should write with such conviction and enthusiasm that a reader who may never have been particularly moved by music thinks, "What have I been missing?" A critic should never write down to that group of readers, but neither should he or she try to impress more musically sophisticated readers with technical displays that could be of interest only to fellow critics and scholars.

Because interviews are also part of the job, music critics must be familiar with the work and outlook of significant music personalities. The ability to be entertaining in such writing, as well as in reviews themselves, is a substantial asset, as long as it is kept in reasonable proportion to the main objective.

The Music Critics Association of North America, the professional organization of American and Canadian critics, considers the education of critics and the establishment of recognized standards to be among its prime objectives. In cooperation with music festivals and universities, the Association has been sponsoring summer institutes and workshops for critics for several years, and it has contacted a number of colleges and universities regarding the possibility of creating a degree program in music (or arts) criticism.

One possible entry into this field is through a related activity, such as broadcasting, program annotation, or public relations work for a musical organization. A more direct way to enter the field is to apply for a position as assistant or junior critic at a newspaper or magazine that has a staff large enough to include such positions or to apply for "stringer" status. Stringers are not staff members but are called in on an as-needed basis to review a particular event. Junior critics, assistants, and stringers are frequently the first to get the nod when a bigger job opens up, either at their own publication or another.

The Internet is another option for music critics. Several Internet sites are now offering music reviews as well as features. There are several advantages to Internet-based writing. There are usually no restrictions on length, as opposed to the shrinking space provided in newspapers, and the article may stay on the site for months. The primary disadvantage at present is that in order to get such exposure, a critic may have to write for little or no compensation.

Once on the ground floor of a large-scale operation, the critic will probably do chores for senior colleagues: writing the daily or weekly calendar of musical events, researching details to accompany the senior critic's major review, keeping the schedule of department assignments, and finding pictures to use with the reviews. These duties acquaint the junior critic with the importance of these details, which the critic on a smaller paper or in a one-person department must look after personally.

Compiled with the assistance of the Music Critics Association of North America.

The Recording Industry

The recording industry consists of some large companies and hundreds of small ones. Regardless of which recording industry specialty you want to pursue, there are some basic skills and personal attributes that you should have. You should have a working knowledge of music, including theory, arranging, and composition. You should be able to adapt your talents to all kinds of music, and you must be reliable when it comes to meeting deadlines and keeping commitments.

In this chapter, you will find descriptions of jobs directly related to the production and distribution of music. For all of these jobs, you should work at becoming a master of your craft and getting to know people who are already in the field.

Recording Musician

Without exception, recording musicians are highly skilled pros who sight-read music and normally give the artist and repertoire (A&R) person (see "Artist and Repertoire [A&R] Person" on page 104), the arranger, the songwriter, or the conductor the right sounds on the first try. The recording musician must be able to cooperate fully, regardless of personal musical style or taste; delays at recording sessions are very expensive and avoided as much as possible. Sometimes musicians will suggest routine or inventive changes, but arguments about arrangements are not tolerated.

The lure of music, the mystique surrounding recording artists and musicians, and the stereotyped fantasies of show business have encouraged a lot of interest in the recording business. But despite the high sales and visibility of the recording industry, job opportunities are not abundant or easy to come by.

While there are several major recording centers in the United States (Los Angeles, New York, Chicago, Nashville, San Francisco, Memphis, Atlanta), there are recording studios throughout the country. The chances of getting that first break are often better in a less competitive community.

In addition, the Internet presents a whole new field of opportunity for new and traditional record companies. It provides record companies with many more distribution opportunities and new ways to expose and distribute their artists' product. In short, the Internet and the advent of digital music mean additional opportunities for recording companies, artists, technology companies, and, of course, consumers.

Skills and Preparation

Preparing for a career as a studio musician means developing excellent performance skills in order to be able to play almost any kind of music after reading the score. To gain experience, one should participate in school music ensembles, join friends in groups, play in family get-togethers, or study music in college.

Those who want to be recording artists should start visiting anyone who might be hiring musicians: recording studios, record companies, publishers, or songwriters. They should leave business cards on the chance that there might be a job available in the future. Sometimes, arrangers and contractors may find that their first-choice musicians are unavailable and call on friends or business associates as substitutes.

There is no formula for breaking into the business or any one technique that will allow one to zoom ahead of the competition—some men and women realize their dreams, but most do not.

Compiled with the assistance of the Recording Industry Association of America.

Producer and Engineer/Mixer

The recording engineer sets up microphones and operates the equipment necessary to record the session according to the instructions of the A&R person (see "Artist and Repertoire [A&R] Person" on page 104). The producer may give presession instructions to the engineer, including a studio floor plan showing instrumental groupings, microphone placement, and the acoustical baffles to be used.

The engineer is concerned with five areas: musical range, rhythm, variety, dynamics, and spectral control. The engineer must be able to compensate for studio limitations, the recording medium, and reproduction equipment.

Skills and Preparation

Because engineering is one of the most popular career areas in recording, studios are extremely selective in hiring. Enrolling in a college that offers specific courses in sound engineering, learning to operate all technical machines, reading the trade magazines, and visiting recording studios is good preparation. It is also good to try to get a studio internship to learn more about the capabilities of the equipment.

Compiled with the assistance of the Recording Industry Association of America.

Studio Arranger

Arrangers can be freelance or affiliated with a particular studio. They score songs for the group and the instruments used in the recording session. The arranger may be a songwriter scoring his or her own works, be a member of a performing group, or work full-time at arranging. Arrangers' fees are set by union contracts based on the number of score pages: the more scores an arranger prepares, the higher the fee. Many arrangers work nights; daytime hours are spent answering inquiries and sometimes conducting.

Skills and Preparation

To become an arranger, it is important to read music quickly and write neatly. It is not necessary to play any instruments well, but it is very important to have a working knowledge of each instrument for which one might be scoring, including their timbres, temperaments, and ranges. A studio arranger also needs a strong sense of what is currently popular and an instinct for future trends.

Compiled with the assistance of the Recording Industry Association of America.

Artist and Repertoire (A&R) Person

The artist and repertoire (A&R) person may be employed by a record company or an artist or may work independently. He or she acts as a liaison between publishers, artists, and record companies, matching songs with musicians to produce a commercially successful sound. Duties include finding new artists, locating fresh material for established singers and groups, hiring arrangers and copyists, preparing the recording session budget, and getting authorization to spend money or raise funds from outside sources.

Skills and Preparation

Major recording companies hire A&R specialists who have proven themselves as successful producers and have demonstrated a talent for creating best-selling recordings. Job advancement in this area depends on the ability to produce results at the point of sale. Working with a promising band that would like to cut a record is a good way to get production experience.

Compiled with the assistance of the Recording Industry Association of America.

Music Copyist

The music copyist transcribes the arranger's score for each musician or group of instruments and may be hired directly by a record company, master producer, arranger, or music department of a film or television production company.

Working hours are very irregular. Fees are set by union contract and vary depending on amount of music, type of instrument, and type of paper used.

Skills and Preparation

Copyists must read music and write legibly, rapidly, and accurately; have a thorough knowledge of music theory and harmony; and be competent with the latest music notation technology. A copyist becomes acquainted with a great deal of music written for the commercial market and will have the chance to meet many influential people in the recording business. Many copyists move on to careers as arrangers.

Compiled with the assistance of the Recording Industry Association of America.

Music Contractor

The music contractor steps in after the A&R (Artist & Repertoire) person (see "Artist and Repertoire [A&R] Person" on page 104) has determined the instrumental and vocal complement for a recording session. The union contractor ensures that all musicians to be called are members of the American Federation of Musicians (AF of M) and that vocalists are members of the American Federation of Television and Radio Artists (AFTRA).

At the session, the contractor is the expert on union rules, settles any problems, makes sure each person receives income tax deduction forms, and files a report of the hours worked and personnel involved with the AF of M and AFTRA.

Hours are often irregular. The union contractor sets the session during business hours and sits in when recordings are made. Some contractors also may participate in sessions as musicians. Therefore, musicians may want to look for producers who are willing to appoint them union contractor.

Skills and Preparation
To qualify, a union contractor must be a musician; a union member; and familiar with contract rules and regulations, performance capabilities and specialties of various musicians in the area, and music preferences of different A&R people.

Compiled with the assistance of the Recording Industry Association of America.

Merchandiser, Manager, Other

In addition to creating and producing records, the recording industry offers many other job opportunities.

The recording industry is oriented to smallness. In almost every job category mentioned here, there are individuals and small independent enterprises that go it alone. Often, these represent the best opportunities for a newcomer to break into the field and eventually become an entrepreneur.

Selling the completed record directly to retailers and wholesalers in a given geographic area is a great way to learn about the business side of the recording industry. It involves appraising product requirements, taking orders, introducing new records, evaluating stock, merchandising the product, and arranging for advertising and merchandising programs.

Merchandising is a sales-support function within a record company that includes developing communication programs to help sell the product and having responsibility for advertising, display, customer communications, sales staff communication, and sales literature.

Promotion in the recording industry usually is geared toward radio and television. Duties are devoted to maximizing the recording's airplay through personal contact with management and broadcast personnel.

Skills and Preparation
Selling is a great way to break into the business. Salespeople often start as part of the junior sales staff or as order or inventory clerks.

background for the prospective DJ. It is also helpful to visit local radio stations to see DJs at work and to learn as much as possible about currently popular artists and songs by listening to recordings and the radio. A prospective DJ should also study the styles of different DJs.

After graduating from college, it is good to first try the smaller stations, which may offer more leeway in music scheduling and programming.

Compiled with the assistance of the Recording Industry Association of America.

Music
Technology

New job opportunities in music technology have been emerging within the past ten to fifteen years. Many of these positions have resulted from new technologies being used in traditional jobs such as music publishing, music copying and printing, arranging, and recording and performing music. Other jobs are a result of totally new applications of technology and digital communication, such as Web publishing, multimedia design, music software design, sound engineering, and Internet-based transmission of music. Indeed, these fast-moving fields hold numerous opportunities for those who want to apply their skills to working with computers, music application software, and digital sound equipment in a music technology career.

Multimedia Publisher

Multimedia Publishing allows access to vast amounts of information on small CD-ROMs, DVD discs, and other electronic media. Those involved in creating these electronic materials include writers, editors, graphic artists, and musicians.

The musician's role in multimedia development is to create original music, arrange existing music for CD-ROM, design "sounds" for effects or audio impact that support the multimedia environment, or organize musical information for publications. Musicians have traditionally been sought out as computer programmers. Musicians with highly developed programming skills can easily secure positions creating multimedia products for publishers and educational institutions.

Skills and Preparation

The value musicians have to multimedia publishers is their understanding of music either as performers, listeners, or composers. Preparation includes a working knowledge of music history, theory, and literature (popular, classical, and jazz). In addition, those hired to create music environments for digital products must have all the skills of a music composer or arranger, plus the ability to operate music synthesizers or other digital keyboards, computer software, MIDI (Musical Instrument Digital Interface) equipment, and sequencers.

For a career as a programmer, one needs to develop skills in using software programs such as multimedia authoring programs, Web development tools, and production software.

Compiled with the assistance of the Music Industry Conference.

Technology-Based Music Instruction Designer

Those with training in music education have been drawn toward the use of computers to enhance music instruction. The use of multimedia in teaching and learning music is a growing field. Several software companies produce multimedia instruction materials for children to learn basic music terminology, performance skills on keyboard and guitar, ear-training skills, music history facts, and numerous additional music skills and knowledge. Designing that software is a growing field in music technology. As the Internet becomes widely available, new software is also emerging as "online," or "distance learning," music instruction.

Skills and Preparation

Obviously, those who plan to design and create high-quality music instruction software must be prepared as teachers. Experience in the music classroom is important. An understanding of learning theory, student motivation, sequencing instruction, instructional models, and student assessment is a major component of preparation. Teachers with an undergraduate degree in music education are prime candidates for such positions as instructional designer, software curriculum consultant, or music technology coordinator. In addition, these professionals should have computer skills in software design, facility with authoring programs and music software, and the ability to manipulate digital sound and video files.

Compiled with the assistance of the Music Industry Conference.

There are many important and fulfilling careers that do not fit into the other categories found in this book. For example, music expertise is required in some specializations within the fields of health care, library science, law, and worship. This chapter illustrates the fact that there is a wide variety of careers in music.

Music Therapist

The use of music to bring about changes in behavior and assist with a variety of functions is known as music therapy. Although it is often thought of as a recent addition to the health care field, music therapy's roots can be traced back to the beginning of recorded civilization. Music and healing have been entwined throughout most of human existence, and the functional role of music in most societies has been equal to, if not paramount to, its artistic role.

Whether one is interested in working with children, the elderly, or persons with learning disabilities, physical disabilities, or emotional illness, music therapy is a recognized treatment for all, and it is used by many health service institutions.

A trained music therapist uses music and music activities to maintain, restore, and improve emotional, cognitive, and physical health. The overall treatment goal is to enable the individual to function more successfully within his or her environment.

Several decades ago, few institutions other than psychiatric hospitals included music therapy in their treatment programs. Gradually, as institutions of all types began examining traditional forms of treatment, more experimentation with alternative methods of treatment was undertaken. Music therapy, one of those alternatives, is now found in a wide variety (and an increasing number) of settings: psychiatric facilities, centers for people with special needs, daycare centers, schools, nursing homes, hospices, prisons, and many others.

Working conditions vary considerably depending on the nature of the facility, the number of patients involved, and the treatment philosophy.

A therapist normally works in one institution with groups of patients, although it may be necessary to work with individuals on a one-to-one basis. Therapy schedules may range from several times a week with small groups to less frequent sessions with larger groups.

Skills and Preparation

Music therapy is a logical career choice for anyone interested in combining music with personal service. To become a music therapist, one should take every opportunity in high school to excel on one's chosen musical instrument and try to get some experience conducting instrumental and vocal groups. A music therapist must not only demonstrate proficiency on his or her major instrument but also become skilled on a variety of other instruments, such as voice, guitar, piano, and recorder. At the least, a music therapist should be able to play piano. Volunteering at local health care facilities is a good way to gain experience. Some students find summer jobs working with children or adults with disabilities in places such as camps or day treatment facilities.

College preparation for a music therapy career mainly focuses on music, psychology, and the social sciences. A standard baccalaureate curriculum has been developed and is offered by more than sixty-five universities. Course work is required in the following areas: music therapy; music psychology; biological, social, and behavioral sciences; disabilities; and general studies. While in college, a prospective music therapist will get experience in clinical practice by observing and conducting activities at treatment facilities.

A master's degree is offered at a number of universities around the country. The minimum requirement for teaching music therapy at the college level is a master's degree plus two years of clinical experience as a therapist.

Following college course work, the therapist will complete a clinical training internship at an approved treatment institution. Successful completion of a music therapy degree and clinical training internship qualifies one to apply for board certification.

Compiled with the assistance of the American Music Therapy Association, Inc.

Music Librarian

Music librarians are musicians in the broadest sense of the word, because music of any style, medium, or era may find a place in a library. They are also librarians. Aptitude and training in both fields are necessary.

Music librarians work in several kinds of libraries. Large music research libraries, such as those at the Library of Congress and the New York Public Library, employ a number of music librarians with comparatively specialized functions. These institutions serve a large public and answer a wide variety of questions, from complex research problems for musicological scholars to the location of obscure or out-of-print music for nationally known concert artists or the person on the street. Librarians in these institutions acquire and integrate every kind of music and everything written about music into their enormous collections.

Large public libraries in major cities frequently have either a separate music, a combination music and art, or a performing arts (including dance and drama) section. Such libraries usually have large circulating collections of recordings in addition to scores and music books.

Even smaller public libraries that cannot employ a music librarian exclusively often have collections of circulating records requiring the supervision of someone with musical knowledge. Also, public libraries often sponsor music recitals or festivals or produce programs for local radio or television.

Most universities, conservatories, and many colleges have separate music libraries headed by professional music librarians. Such libraries usually offer research and reference facilities and circulating collections, including scores and performing parts.

A university music librarian works with the faculty to develop a library that meets the needs of students and provides more literature and information for the advanced or curious student. He or she also cooperates with performing ensembles in the school, often helping orchestras, opera workshop presenters, or chamber ensembles find the music they require.

Certain special libraries also serve the music field. Radio and television stations may have their own libraries. Large music publishers and organizations, such as the American Society of Composers, Authors, and Publishers (ASCAP), sometimes hire music librarians to organize and deal with their holdings. Music retailers, too, often find library training valuable in their profession.

Orchestra librarians, whose main function is to acquire instrumental works for an orchestra and prepare them for performance, occupy a somewhat special category in that they are not usually professional librarians. For this job, the ability to read and write music fluently and legibly is more important than the reference and cataloging skills used by other music librarians.

Because music libraries are comparatively small and specialized to begin with, music librarians often have to assume several different functions: administrator; reference specialist; and liaison with the public, faculty, and library staff.

Only the music cataloger is likely to work within a rather restricted sphere. The cataloger generally works alone, preparing catalog entries and subject headings and classifying new material according to the system used in a particular library. Cataloging can be an intellectually challenging task if there is a variety of material to be considered.

Outside of large research libraries, most institutions do not employ more than two or three music librarians, with a cataloger and perhaps a recording specialist to assist the head music librarian. Salaries are not high.

The field is not large and there is a consequent lack of mobility in the higher positions. Attractive openings are not always easy to find, especially if geographical considerations are important. Most jobs are located in cities or in college and university communities. Some of these, New York for example, are more popular than others. Even excellent qualifications do not always guarantee a specific position.

On the positive side, music librarianship can be consistently interesting to the intellectually curious person. Routine tasks are constantly varied by the changing needs of the library and its patrons. Music librarians come in contact with many areas and aspects of music; a few minutes of a librarian's day may include helping a young flute student, a local opera director, a Japanese koto player, and a teenage fan of country fiddling. This is a position that serves student and teacher, professional and amateur, composer and critic. Like many people in the music field, music librarians frequently participate in other musical activities in their spare time. Many music librarians are also performers, composers, critics, or musicologists.

Skills and Preparation

As librarianship is essentially an academic pursuit, intellectual curiosity and competence are requisites for success. People in the technical services connected with libraries, such as cataloging, often work behind the scenes. Most music librarians, however, work with people, so a confident, outgoing personality is definitely an asset.

Training for music librarianship should include as broad an education as possible in all aspects of music and liberal arts, supplemented by graduate training in librarianship. Most successful music librarians did not choose this field early in their schooling because, although it is rather small, the background required is immense, and only a student of varied interests is likely to accumulate the kind of knowledge a good music librarian needs. Graduate study, including a thorough course in music bibliography, is desirable. In many positions, a second master's degree (in addition to the library science master's) or a Ph.D. in musicology is required. Experience as a performing musician also is valuable; it gives the librarian practical experience in the requirements of many library users and acquaints him or her more intimately with a specific musical repertoire.

Because information about music and musical editions is likely to be published in any country and in any language, music librarians should also have working knowledge of German and at least one Romance language to do the most basic cataloging or bibliographic research. In addition to languages and the history of literature of music, the undergraduate should study a wide variety of liberal arts, history, literature, art, and philosophy, because music librarians need to be able to draw on information and resources from other disciplines as well as their own specialties.

Because of the knowledge to be accumulated, formal training in librarianship usually comes rather late in the educational process. Most accredited schools of library science offer graduate programs of at least thirty-six credits, culminating in the Master of Library Science degree, which is required for most professional jobs. These programs offer training in theory and practice of librarianship, bibliography, reference, acquisition, cataloging, and administration. Some schools offer special courses in music librarianship or joint programs in music and librarianship. While these can be very valuable, there is no shortcut to acquiring the knowledge a music librarian needs to have.

The best way to find out if this might be an interesting, satisfying career is to work part-time in a library. Libraries usually have places for college or high school students to help shelve books and perform minor clerical tasks. Knowledge of typing is helpful for advancement at the clerical level, but simply being in and part of the library will acquaint one with many of its operations. Working hours are usually flexible and conditions are pleasant for those who like books; many students use the opportunity to earn extra money even if they have no plans to stay in library work. Practical experience working in a library also can be invaluable for library school.

Compiled with the assistance of the Music Library Association.

Music Industry Attorney

In an increasingly complex music marketplace, the music industry attorney handles many aspects of the music business, including, but not limited to, intellectual property contract provisions, copyright, trademark, rights of publication, reproduction, distribution and public performance rights, as well as union agreements, publishing contracts, independent record production distribution, methods of accounting, retail promotion, artist and management agreements, videocassettes and other audiovisual media, and the Internet. In addition, music industry attorneys try to handle all nonmusic business and personal legal matters in order to provide full-time service to their entertainment clients.

Skills and Preparation

Naturally a music industry attorney must become a lawyer first, but to specialize in music-related law, it helps to learn the business of music early on. The music industry attorney must be familiar with all of the aspects of the music business that are listed above.

There is no right way to get started. Knocking on doors, being persistent, and being creative are all necessary. A resume for a music industry attorney should be direct and simple, but one should not overlook creative ways to enter a creative business.

Compiled with the assistance of the American Society of Composers, Authors, and Publishers (ASCAP), and Broadcast Music, Inc. (BMI).

Worship Musician

Careers in the field of music for worship can be as numerous and varied as places of worship themselves. However, one thing is common to all: These career opportunities give musicians the chance to lead others in music making and, through music, help the church enrich people's lives.

Budgets and job openings for full-time musicians at places of worship are increasingly available. Those who pursue full-time or even part-time careers in this field seem to find such work challenging and satisfying.

Just as denominations differ, churches and synagogues within a given denomination or tradition can be very different from one another. Church choral programs can vary from a huge multiple-choir setup involving 1,200 volunteer singers in one church to the sophisticated, paid men-and-boy-choir programs found in a metropolitan church, to a small folk group in another church.

More and more, musicians seem to be veering away from exclusive reliance on the four-part, chorus-and-organ sound traditionally associated with church music. Many new anthems and hymns call for unusual accompaniments or no accompaniment at all. There is more use of unison singing, choir and congregational refrain songs, and auxiliary instruments, which provide variety and varied musical textures. Many institutions of worship find that purely musical programs, above and beyond the regular church services, are a rewarding and enjoyable way for the church to make contact with people in the community.

Some churches and synagogues employ full-time *music directors*. These directors have ultimate responsibility for all music required by the congregation and may have help in the form of an assistant who serves as organist. In other institutions, the *choirmaster* also serves as organist. A church *organist,* in addition to playing regular services and extra musical programs for the community, will play for special services, such as weddings and funerals. These events can help supplement his or her income.

Skills and Preparation

To get started in a religious music career, one should talk to organists, choir directors, instrumentalists, or liturgists in the community. Their experience and advice can be invaluable in helping know what direction to take.

A church musician must possess talent and technique and the drive and self-discipline to put them to work. He or she also needs to be skilled in human relations.

A choir director in a religious institution needs a thorough understanding and knowledge of music fundamentals (harmony, theory, counterpoint), the workings of the human voice, and choral and instrumental conducting. He or she must be familiar with both old and new choral and organ repertoire, liturgical structure, hymnody, and history. Regardless of a choir director's denomination or tradition, it is important to understand all music traditions, from Gregorian chant to current rock music. A basic keyboard facility is also required.

An organist should have an understanding of the organ and its literature. Recital or solo playing, leading a congregation in singing, and accompanying choirs and soloists all require different skills. It is possible for a gifted recitalist to be a poor service player and vice versa. Organists need a feel for worship to lift it above the limitations of mere language and tie together the different parts of a service. The ability to improvise can be an important asset. This ability can be developed—to a point—in almost any organist, although some will show greater skill than others. Outside of progressive jazz, there is probably no area where improvisation can be used to such advantage.

Anyone considering the field of music for worship should get involved in as many musical activities as possible in high school and at the local church or synagogue. It is also wise to take private vocal and instrumental lessons and sing in a school or church choral group. Looking for chances to conduct others and play in an instrumental ensemble, trying to develop a sharper sense of rhythm and pitch, and training the ear to hear musical sounds and detect subtle differences in music is the best way to prepare for this career.

For further preparation, one may want to attend a college, university, or music school specializing in music for worship (a degree is necessary if one is looking for a job at a major church or synagogue). It is also important to get practical experience in leading or accompanying music in actual services. Many colleges not only offer but require field experience as part of their curriculum. Such experience sometimes enables a student to earn a small salary while learning and helping out at a place of worship.

Education in music for worship and related subjects should continue even after formal schooling is complete. Musicians should keep current with what is happening in all church traditions, as well as in their own denominations. That will enable them to make a greater, more knowledgeable contribution to their own religious group.

Workshops, seminars, and courses to further education exist throughout the country. In late fall, church music journals begin listing summer courses.

Compiled with the assistance of the American Guild of Organists, the Church Music Association of America, and the National Association of Pastoral Musicians.

Directory of Music-Related Information Sources

Directory of Music-Related Information Sources

American Bandmasters Association, 1521 South Pickard, Norman, OK
    73072; 405-321-3373; thurston3@juno.com;
    http://www.tntech.edu/www/aba/index.htm

American Choral Directors Association, 502 SW 38th Street, Lawton, OK
    73505; 580-355-8161; acda@acdaonline.org; http://www.acdaonline.org

American Choral Foundation, c/o Chorus America, 1156 15th Street NW,
    Suite 310, Washington, DC 20005; 202-331-7577;
    service@chorusamerica.org; http://www.chorusamerica.org

American Federation of Musicians of the United States and Canada, AFL-
    CIO, 1501 Broadway, Suite 600, New York, NY 10036; 212-869-1330;
    info@afm.org; http://www.afm.org

American Federation of Television and Radio Artists (AFTRA), 260
    Madison Avenue, 7th floor New York, NY 10016; 212-532-0800;
    aftra@aftra.com; http://www.aftra.com

American Guild of Organists, 475 Riverside Drive, Suite 1260, New York,
    NY 10115; 212-870- 2310; info@agohq.org; http://www.agohq.org

American Music Conference, 5790 Armada Drive, Carlsbad, CA 92008;
    619-431-9124; info@amc-music.com; http://www.amc-music.com

American Orff-Schulwerk Association, P.O. Box 391089, Cleveland, OH
    44139-8089; 440-543-5366; hdqtrs@aosa.com; http://www.aosa.org

American School Band Directors Association, P.O. Box 696, Guttenberg,
    IA 52052; 319-252-2383; asbda@netins.net; http://www.asbda.com

American Society of Composers, Authors, and Publishers (ASCAP), One
    Lincoln Plaza, New York, NY 10023; 212-621-6000; info@ascap.com;
    http://www.ascap.com

American Society of Music Copyists, P.O. Box 2557, Times Square
    Station, New York, NY 10108; ASMC802@aol.com;
    http://members.aol.com/asmc802/home.htm

American String Teachers Association with National School Orchestra

Association, 1806 Robert Fulton Drive, Suite 300, Reston, VA 20191; 703-476-1316; asta@erols.com; http://www.astaweb.com/

American Symphony Orchestra League, 1156 15th Street NW, Suite 805, Washington, DC 20005; 202-776-0212; league@symphony.org; http://www.symphony.org

Aspen Music Festival and School, 2 Music School Road, Aspen, CO 81611; 970-925-3254; fax 970-925-3802; festival@aspenmusic.org; http://www.aspenmusicfestival.com

Association of Performing Arts Presenters, 1112 16th Street NW, Suite 400, Washington, DC 20036; 202-833-2787; artspres@presenters.org; http://www.artspresenters.org

Association for Technology in Music Instruction, c/o Peter Webster, School of Music, Northwestern University, 633 Clark Street, Evanston, IL 60208; 847-491-5740; pwebster@nwu.edu; http://www.music.org/atmi

Audio Engineering Society, 60 East 42nd Street, Room 2520, New York, NY 10165; 212-661-8528; hq@aes.org; http://www.aes.org

Broadcast Music, Inc. (BMI), 320 W. 57th Street, New York, NY 10019; 212-586-2000; newyork@bmi.com; http://www.bmi.com

Chamber Music America, 305 Seventh Avenue, New York, NY 10001; 212-242-2022; info@chamber-music.org; http://www.chamber-music.org

Church Music Association of America, c/o Kurt Poterack, Ph.D., 875 Malta N.E., Grand Rapids, MI 49503; 616-451-3780; 105066.1540@compuserve.com

College Band Directors National Association, c/o Richard L. Floyd, MSC 8028, University of Texas, Austin, TX 78713; 512-471-5883; webmaster@cbdna.org; http://www.cbdna.org

The College Music Society, 202 W. Spruce, Missoula, MT 59802; 406-721-9616; cms@music.org; http://www.music.org

Conductors Guild, Inc., North Lakeside Cultural Center, 6219 N. Sheridan Rd., Chicago, IL 60660; 773-764-7563; conguild@aol.com; http://www.conductorsguild.org

Guild of American Luthiers, 8222 South Park Avenue Tacoma, WA 98408; phone & fax: 253-472-7853; http://www.luth.org

Guitar and Accessories Marketing Association, c/o Jerry Hershman, 40 West 21st Street, Room 1106, New York, NY 10010-6906; 212-924-9175; assnhdqs@aol.com

Interlochen Center for the Arts, P.O. Box 199, Interlochen, MI 49643-0199; 231-276-7200; academy@interlochen.k12.mi.us; http://www.interlochen.org

International Association of Electronic Keyboard Manufacturers, c/o Jerry Hershman, 40 West 21st Street, Room 1106, New York, NY

10010-6906; 212-924-9175; assnhdqs@aol.com;
http://www.iaekm.org

MENC: The National Association for Music Education, 1806 Robert
Fulton Drive, Reston, VA 20191; 703-860-4000; elizabet@menc.org;
http://www.menc.org

Music Critics Association of North America, 7 Pine Court, Westfield, NJ
07090; 908-789-1515; brdh97@prodigy.com

Music Distributors Association, c/o Jerry Hershman, 38 West 21st Street,
Room 1106, New York, NY 10010-6906; 212-924-9175;
assnhdqs@aol.com; http://www.musicdistributors.org

Music Industry Conference, 1806 Robert Fulton Drive, Reston, VA 20191;
703-860-4000; sandraf@menc.org; http://www.menc.org

Music Library Association, 6707 Old Dominion Dr., Suite 315, McLean,
VA 22101; 703-556- 8780; soderwald@kimbal.com;
http://www.musiclibraryassoc.org

Music Publishers' Association of the United States, PMB 246, 1562 First
Avenue, New York, NY 10028; 212-327-4044; mpa-admin@mpa.org;
http://www.mpa.org

Music Teachers National Association, The Carew Tower, 441 Vine Street,
Suite 505, Cincinnati, OH 45202-2814; 513-421-1420;
mtnanet@mtna.org; http://www.mtna.org

National Academy of Recording Arts and Sciences (NARAS), 3402 Pico
Blvd., Santa Monica, CA 90405; 310-392-3777;
http://www.grammy.com

National Association of Band Instrument Manufacturers, c/o Jerry
Hershman, 40 West 21st Street, Room 1106, New York, NY 10010-
6906; 212-924-9175; assnhdqs@aol.com

National Association of Broadcast Employees and Technicians, 501 Third
Street, NW, Washington, DC 20001-2797; 202-434-1254; fax: 202-434-
1426; nabet@nabetcwa.org; http://union.nabetcwa.org/nabet

National Association of Broadcasters, 1771 N Street NW, Washington, DC
20036; 202-429-5300; ssiroky@nab.org; http://www.nab.org

National Association of College Wind and Percussion Instructors, c/o Dr.
Richard Weerts, Division of Fine Arts, Truman State University, 100
East Normal Street, Kirksville, MO 63501; 660-785-4442;
fa24@truman.edu

National Association of Composers/USA, P.O. Box 49256, Barrington
Station, Los Angeles, CA 90049; 310-541-8213; nacusa@music-
usa.org; http://www.music-usa.org/nacusa

NAMM: International Music Products Association, 5790 Armada Drive,
Carlsbad, CA 92008; 760-438-8001; info@amc-music.com;
http://www.amc-music.com

National Association for Music Therapy, 8455 Colesville Road, Suite 1000, Silver Spring, MD 20910-3319; 301-589-3300; info@musictherapy.org; http://www.musictherapy.org

National Association of Professional Band Instrument Repair Technicians, P.O. Box 51, Normal, IL 61761; 309-452-4257; chagler@napbirt.org; http://www.napbirt.org

National Association of Teachers of Singing, Inc., 6406 Merril Road, Suite B, Jacksonville, Florida 32277; 904-744-9022; info@nats.org; http://www.nats.org

National Association of Recording Merchandisers, 9 Eves Drive, Suite 120, Marlton, NJ 08053; 856-596-2221; goffin@narm.com; http://www.narm.com

National Association of School Music Dealers, 4020 McEwen, Suite 10, Dallas, TX 75244-5041; 972-233-9107; mad@dondillon.com; http://www.nasmd.com

National Association of Schools of Music, 11250 Roger Bacon Drive #21, Reston, VA 20190; 703-437-0700; info@arts-accredit.org; http://www.arts-accredit.org

National Band Association, P.O. Box 121292, Nashville, TN 37212; 615-385-2650; nbassoc@bellsouth.net; http://www.nationalbandassoc.org

National Council of Music Importers and Exporters, 38 West 21st Street, Room 1106, New York, NY 10011; 212-924-9175; assnhdqs@aol.com

National Music Council, c/o Dr. David Sanders, 425 Park Street, Upper Montclair, NJ 07043; phone: 973-655-7974; fax 973-655-5432; sandersd@saturn.montclair.edu; http://www.musiccouncil.org

National Music Publishers Association, Inc.,The Harry Fox Agency, 711 Third Ave., New York, NY 10017; 212-370-5330; clientservice@harryfox.com; http://www.harryfox.com

National Orchestral Association, 475 Riverside Drive, Room 249, New York, NY 10027; 212-350-4676

National Piano Foundation, 4020 McEwen #105, Dallas, TX 75244-5041; 972-233-9107; info@pianonet.com; http://www.pianonet.com

National Symphony Orchestra Association, JFK Center for the Performing Arts, 2700 F Street, Washington, DC 20566; 202-416-8000; http://www.kennedy-center.org/nso

Navy Music Program, NPC-64, Navy Personnel Command, 5720 Integrity Drive, Millington, TN 38055; 901-874-4312; p64f@persnet.navy.mil; http://www.persnet.navy.mil

Organization of American Kodály Educators, P.O. Box 9804, Fargo, ND 58106-9804; 701-235- 0366; oake-mail@corpcomm.net; http://www.oake.org

Piano Manufacturers Association International, 4020 McEwen #105,

Dallas, TX 75244-5041; 972-233-9107; don@dondillon.com
Piano Technicians Guild, Inc., 3930 Washington Street, Kansas City, MO
   64111-2963; 816-753-7747; ptg@ptg.org; http://www.ptg.org
Recording Industry Association of America, 1330 Connecticut Ave. NW,
   Suite 300, Washington, DC 20036; 202-775-0101; http://www.riaa.com
Retail Print Music Dealers Association, 4020 McEwen #105, Dallas, TX
   75244-5019; 972-233-9107; office@printmusic.org;
   http://www.printmusic.org
SESAC, Inc., 55 Music Square East, Nashville, TN 37203; 615-320-0055;
   ccaviness@sesac.com; http://www.sesac.com
The Songwriters Guild of America, 1500 Harbor Blvd., Weehawken, NJ
   07087-6732; 201-867-7603; lasga@aol.com;
   http://www.songwriters.org
Suzuki Association of the Americas, Inc., P.O. Box 17310, Boulder, CO
   80308; 303-444-0948; suzuki@rmi.net;
   http://www.suzukiassociation.org
Tanglewood Music Center, Boston Symphony Hall, 301 Massachusetts
   Ave., Boston, MA 02115; 617-266-1492; tmc@bso.org;
   http://www.bso.org
United States Air Force Bands Division, Office of Public Affairs
   (SAF/PAB), 1690 Air Force Pentagon, Washington, DC 20330-1690;
   703-696-9165; Virgil.Layne@pentagon.af.mil;
   http://www.af.mil/band/home.htm
United States Army Band, Public Affairs Office, 204 Lee Avenue, Fort
   Myer, VA 22211-1199; 703-696-3718 (to hotline: 703-696-3399);
   corcorang@fmmc.army.mil; http://www.army.mil/armyband
United States Coast Guard Band, Public Affairs Office, U.S. Coast Guard
   Academy, 15 Mohegan Avenue (pb), New London, CT 06320-4195;
   860-701-6810; cpo_e_gibbs@unixlink.uscga.edu;
   http://www.cga.edu/band/default.html
United States Marine Band ("The President's Own"), Attn; Operations
   Officer, Marine Barracks, 8th and I Streets SE, Washington, DC 20390-
   5000; 202-433-5809; hurleyj@hqi.usmc.mil;
   http://www.marineband.usmc.mil
Volunteer Lawyers for the Arts, 1 E. 53rd Street, 6th Floor, New York, NY
   10022; 212-319-2787; vlany@busy.net; http://www.stus.com
Women Band Directors International; c/o Dr. Susan D. Creasap, president;
   Baird Music Hall, Morehead State University, Morehead, KY 40351;
   http://www.WBDI.org

Other MENC Career Materials

A Career Guide to Music Education (online publication). Practical information for the music education student. This publication includes job search tips, information about resume development, interview strategies, and advice about graduate education. Available at http://www.menc.org.

Careers in Music, rev. (online publication). A concise summary of a wide range of music careers. Includes information such as skill and education requirements, employment opportunities, and average salaries. Available at http://www.menc.org.

Careers in Music (video). Through footage taken at Grammy® In the Schools Days, this video provides an introduction to the program and an overview of the various opportunities available in the music industry. Produced by National Academy of Recording Arts & Sciences. 1991. VHS. 62 minutes. Stock #3057.

Teacher Success Kit: How to Succeed in Music Education (CD-ROM). A computer diskette loaded with information to help music teachers succeed in the classroom. Contains helpful tips from elementary teachers; secondary chorus, band, and orchestra teachers; and music supervisors. 1999. Stock # 3101.

For complete ordering information on these and other publications, contact:

MENC Publication Sales
1806 Robert Fulton Drive
Reston, VA 20191-4348
Credit card holders may call 1-800-828-0229.